A DICTIONARY OF NARRATOLOGY

Gerald Prince

Dictionary of Narratology

UNIVERSITY OF NEBRASKA PRESS: LINCOLN & LONDON

The paper in this book meets
the minimum require-
ments of American National
Standard for Infor-
mation Sciences – Permanence
of Paper for
Printed Library Materials,
ANSI Z39.48–1984.

Library of Congress Cataloging
in Publication Data

Prince, Gerald.
A dictionary of narratology.

Bibliography: p.
1. Discourse analysis, Narrative – Dictionaries.
I. Title.
P302.7.P75   1987
808.3′00141   87–4998
ISBN 0-8032-3678-6
alkaline paper

Contents

Preface

In this dictionary, I define, explain, and illustrate terms that are specific to narratology (e.g., *narreme, extradiegetic*); terms whose narratological acceptation differs from their other ones (e.g., *voice, transformation*); and terms whose "ordinary" or technical meaning belongs to a semantic domain that is prominent in or essential to narratological description and argumentation (e.g., *code, rewrite rule*).

My list is not exhaustive. I have retained only terms that enjoy wide currency in narratology—terms that are used and can be used by narratologists with different theoretical or methodological preferences—as well as a few terms that I consider helpful and that might gain currency and a few other terms that are no longer very fashionable but once were. Furthermore, I have concentrated on terms used in connection with verbal rather than nonverbal narratives: I believe that this bias reflects the biases of narratology itself. I have attempted not to neglect any important movement: I have drawn on the Anglo-Saxon tradition originating with Henry James and Percy Lubbock, the German tradition of Lämmert or Stanzel, the Russian Formalists and the Russian semioticians, the French structuralists, and the Tel Aviv poeticians; I have taken into account the narratological labors of linguists, psychologists, anthropologists, historians, and students of artificial intelligence; and I have not forgotten Aristotle. Nevertheless, I have been partial to what constitutes perhaps the most influential narratological work of the past twenty years, that of "French" or "French-inspired" narratologists. Finally, I have left out a large number of terms which are no doubt pertinent to the analysis of narrative but which I regard as belonging more appropriately in dictionaries of rhetoric, semiotics, linguistics, or literature (e.g., *cooperative principle* and *allegory* or *novel* and *romance*).

If my list of terms is not exhaustive, neither are my explanations of these terms complete. In the first place, I have not attempted to provide a thorough survey of definitions of or opinions on any given term; rather, I have sought to provide an overview, and I have given what I consider to be the most important and useful definitions or opinions. In the second place, I have repeatedly opted for short formulations, in the belief that a dictionary should (and can) only be a helpful starting point. (The few cases in which I have supplied more lengthy formulations are intended to suggest the richness of the discussions that a particular term and the notions it designates have provoked.) I have tried to keep technical language to a minimum, and I have been spare with examples (paradoxically, they often lead to confusion rather than clarification); but I have not avoided repetitions, since I have a lot of faith in their pedagogical effectiveness.

The terms selected are presented in a single alphabetical listing. I have made generous use of cross-references, in spite of the anxiety they might create, to indicate relations, parallels, and contexts and to point to further examples or clarifications: when a term characterized in the dictionary appears in the body of an entry, it is printed in SMALL CAPITALS. The few exceptions to this practice pertain to such recurrent terms as *narrator* or *character:* a cross-reference seemed, at times, superfluous. Furthermore, whenever I thought that the characterization (or knowledge) of one or more other terms in the dictionary would enrich the user's understanding of a particular entry, I have added a statement of the form "See also SUCH AND SUCH" at the very end of the entry. I have also given bibliographical references at the end of most entries in order to allow the user of the dictionary to investigate the topics further and in order to identify at least some of the sources on which my formulations are based. Again, the few exceptions to this practice— e.g., *conjoining, constitutional model, mediator*—are cases where the context, cross-references, and/or cross-referential statements make bibliographical indications superfluous. When an entry has two or more definitions (e.g., *competence, contact, plot*) and if pertinent, the formulation of the subentries points to the bibliographical item(s) that are particularly relevant to each definition. The references are collected in the bibliography to be found at the end of the volume.

When I started to prepare this dictionary, I wanted it to give a sense of narratology as a discipline and to constitute a space for indicating some of the agreements, compatibilities, and divergences obtaining in a field that has undergone remarkable growth since the 1960s and the heyday of structuralism. I also—and even more so—wanted it to constitute a simple guide to many of the terms, concepts, and ambitions characterizing narratological study as well as a stimulant to the development, sharpening, and refining of narratological tools. I hope that I have been at least partly successful.

I would like to thank the University of Pennsylvania for granting me a leave in the fall of 1985 which allowed me to write much of this dictionary. I would also like to thank Ellen F. Prince for patient and invaluable suggestions. I feel indebted to the readers of the manuscript for the University of Nebraska Press: their comments were of great benefit.

A

abruptive dialogue. A DIALOGUE in which the speakers' utterances are not accompanied by TAG CLAUSES: "—How are you today? —I feel great! and you? —I feel fine." ¶Genette 1980.

absent narrator. A maximally COVERT NARRATOR; an IMPERSONAL NARRATOR; a narrator presenting situations and events with minimum narratorial mediation and in no way referring to a narrating self or a narrating activity. Absent narrators are characteristic of BEHAVIORIST NARRATIVES ("Hills Like White Elephants"). ¶Chatman 1978. See also MEDIATED NARRATION, NONNARRATED NARRATIVE, SHOWING.

abstract. The part of a NARRATIVE which summarizes it and encapsulates its POINT, or main thrust. If a narrative is taken to constitute a series of answers to certain questions, the abstract is that constituent of it answering the questions "What was this narrative about?" and "Why was this narrative told?" ¶Labov 1972; Pratt 1977.

achronic structure. A sequence of events, as opposed to an isolated event or two, characterized by ACHRONY (cf. Marcel's walks toward Méséglise and toward Guermantes in the first part of *Remembrance of Things Past*). ¶Genette 1980. See also ORDER, SYLLEPSIS.

achrony. An event deprived of any temporal connection with other events; a dateless event. Robbe-Grillet's *Jealousy* abounds in achronies. ¶Bal 1985; Genette 1980. See also ACHRONIC STRUCTURE, ORDER.

act. 1. Along with the HAPPENING, one of two possible kinds of narrated EVENTS; a change of state brought about by an AGENT and manifested in discourse by a PROCESS STATEMENT in the mode of *do;* an ACTION. "Mary solved the problem" represents an act, whereas "It rained yesterday" does not. **2.** A syntagmatic constituent of an action, an action being made up of several acts. ¶Chatman 1978; Greimas and Courtés 1982. See also NARRATIVE STATEMENT.

actant. A fundamental ROLE at the level of narrative DEEP STRUCTURE (corresponding to Souriau's FUNCTION, Propp's DRAMATIS PERSONA, and Lotman's ARCHIPERSONA). The term was introduced into narratology by Greimas, following the linguist Tesnière, who had used it to designate a type of syntactic unit. By reworking the role typologies proposed by Souriau and Propp, Greimas arrived at an ACTANTIAL MODEL originally consisting of six actants: SUBJECT (Souriau's LION, Propp's HERO), OBJECT (Souriau's SUN, Propp's SOUGHT-FOR PERSON), SENDER (Souriau's BALANCE, Propp's DISPATCHER), RECEIVER (Souriau's EARTH), HELPER (Souriau's MOON, Propp's HELPER and DONOR), and OPPONENT (Souriau's

1

MARS, Propp's VILLAIN and FALSE HERO). In a more recent version of Greimas's actantial model, Helper and Opponent are taken to be AUXILIANTS and not actants. ¶An actant can occupy a certain number of specified positions or ACTANTIAL ROLES along its NARRATIVE TRAJECTORY. The Subject, for instance, can be established as such by the Sender, qualified (made competent) along the axis of ability, realized as a successful performer, and rewarded for its performance. Furthermore, at the level of narrative SURFACE STRUCTURE, one actant can be represented by several different ACTORS, and several actants can be represented by one and the same actor. Thus, in an adventure story, the Subject may have several enemies, all of whom function as Opponent; and in a simple love story, the boy may function as both Subject and Receiver while the girl functions as both Object and Sender. Finally, not only human actors but also animals, things, and concepts can fulfill the fundamental roles constituting the actantial model: a diamond can represent the Object of the Subject's quest and an ideological imperative can function as the Sender. ¶Though the term *actant* is most often used with reference to the basic roles that are played by entities in the world of the situations and events recounted, it is also used sometimes to refer to the roles of NARRATOR and NARRATEE: these are actants of communication as opposed to actants of narration (Subject, Object, Sender, or Receiver). ¶Courtés 1976; Culler 1975; Greimas 1970, 1983a, 1983b; Greimas and Courtés 1982; Hamon 1972; Hénault 1983;

Scholes 1974. See also CHARACTER.

actantial model. The structure of relations obtaining among ACTANTS. According to Greimas, narrative is a signifying whole because it can be grasped in terms of such a structure. ¶The original actantial model involved six actants: SUBJECT (looking for the OBJECT), Object (looked for by the Subject), SENDER (of the Subject on its quest for the Object), RECEIVER (of the Object to be secured by the Subject), HELPER (of the Subject), and OPPONENT (of the Subject). It is often represented by the following diagram:

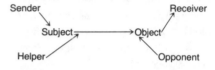

In accounting for the actantial structure of *Madame Bovary,* for instance, the model might yield something like this: *Subject*—Emma; *Object*—happiness; *Sender*—Romantic literature; *Receiver*—Emma; *Helper*—Léon, Rodolphe; *Opponent*—Charles, Yonville, Rodolphe, Homais, Lheureux. ¶A more recent version of the model involves only four actants: Subject, Object, Sender, and Receiver (with Helper and Opponent functioning as AUXILIANTS). ¶Adam 1984; Courtés 1976; Culler 1975; Greimas 1970, 1983a, 1983b.

actantial role. A formal position occupied by an ACTANT along its NARRATIVE TRAJECTORY; a particular state assumed by an actant in the logical unfolding of a narrative. In its trajectory, for example, the SUBJECT is instituted as such by the SENDER and can be modalized (qualified, made competent) along the axes of desire, ability, knowledge, and obligation, realized as a performing Subject, recognized as one, and rewarded. ¶The different actantial roles in a given trajectory are sufficiently autonomous to be incarnated by different ACTORS. In other words, the actant, which constitutes a fundamental role at the DEEP STRUCTURE level, is specified through a series of actantial roles along a narrative trajectory and further specified as one or more actors at the SURFACE STRUCTURE level. ¶Chabrol 1973; Greimas 1970, 1983a; Greimas and Courtés 1982; Hénault 1983. See also AUXILIANT, MODALITY, THEMATIC ROLE.

action. **1.** A series of connected events exhibiting unity and significance and moving through a BEGINNING, a MIDDLE, and an END; a syntagmatic organization of ACTS. In Aristotelian terms, an action is a process from bad to good fortune or the reverse. Two actions can, of course, constitute a larger action. **2.** In Barthes's terminology, a group of FUNCTIONS subsumed under the same ACTANT(s): for instance, functions involving the SUBJECT in its movement toward the OBJECT would constitute the action we call QUEST **3.** An act. ¶Aristotle 1968; Barthes 1975; Brooks and Warren 1959; Chatman 1978; Genot 1979; Greimas and Courtés 1982.

actor. The concretization of an ACTANT at the level of narrative SURFACE STRUCTURE. The actor, which results from the conjunction of at least one ACTANTIAL ROLE and one THEMATIC ROLE, is represented by a unit equivalent to a noun phrase and individuated in such a way as to constitute an autonomous figure of the narrative world. ¶The actor need not appear as an anthropomorphic being: it might, for instance, take the shape of a flying carpet, a table, or a corporation. Moreover, the actor can be individual (John, Mary) or collective (a subway crowd), figurative (anthropomorphic, zoomorphic, etc.) or nonfigurative (Fate). Finally, one actor can represent several different actants, and several actors can represent one and the same actant. In romances, for example, the protagonist often functions as both SUBJECT and RECEIVER; and in adventure stories, the various enemies of the hero or heroine all function as OPPONENT. ¶Adam 1985; Greimas 1970, 1983a, 1983b; Greimas and Courtés 1982; Hénault 1983; Mathieu 1974; Scholes 1974. See also CHARACTER.

actorial narrative type. The class of HOMODIEGETIC or HETERODIEGETIC NARRATIVES characterized by INTERNAL FOCALIZATION *(Hunger, The Ambassadors)*. Along with the AUCTORIAL and the NEUTRAL NARRATIVE TYPES, it is one of three basic classes in Lintvelt's typology. ¶Genette 1983; Lintvelt 1981. See also POINT OF VIEW.

addressee. One of the fundamental constituents of any act of (verbal) communication: the (intended) RECEIVER, the ENUNCIATEE. The addressee receives a MESSAGE from the ADDRESSER. ¶K. Bühler 1934; Jakobson 1960. See also CONATIVE FUNCTION, CONSTITUTIVE FACTORS OF COMMUNICATION.

addresser. One of the fundamental constituents of any act of (verbal) communication: the SENDER, the ENUNCIATOR. The addresser sends a MESSAGE to the ADDRESSEE. ¶K. Bühler 1934; Jakobson 1960. See also

advance mention. A narrative element the significance of which becomes clear only (well) after it is first mentioned; a narrative "seed" the importance of which is not recognized when it first appears. A character is casually introduced in the first chapter of a novel, for example, and begins to play a decisive role only in chapter 20; an ordinary living-room couch is mentioned in passing and, very much later, turns out to conceal crucial secrets; the mere opening of a window proves to have incalculable consequences after a year goes by. ¶The advance mention is not to be confused with the ADVANCE NOTICE. The former does not constitute an example of PROLEPSIS; the latter does. The former in no way refers or alludes to what will happen; the latter does so explicitly. ¶Genette 1980. See also FORESHADOWING.

advance notice. A narrative unit referring in advance to situations and events that will occur and be recounted at a later point; a repeating PROLEPSIS; an ANTICIPATION: "That I was one day to experience a grief as profound as that of my mother, we shall see in the course of this narrative"; "We shall see also that, on the contrary, the Duchesse de Guermantes did associate with Odette and Gilberte after the death of Swann." ¶Genette 1980. See also ADVANCE MENTION, ANACHRONY.

agent. **1.** A human or humanized being performing an ACTION or ACT; a CHARACTER who acts and influences the course of events. **2.** Along with the PATIENT, one of two fundamental ROLES in Bremond's typology. Whereas patients are affected by certain processes, agents initiate these processes and, more specifically, influence the patients, modify their situation (improving or worsening it), or maintain it (for the good or the bad). In the set of influencers, we find informers and dissimulators, seducers and intimidators, obligators and interdictors; in the set of modifiers, we find improvers and degraders; in the set of maintainers, we find protectors and frustrators. ¶Bremond 1973; van Dijk 1973; Scholes 1974; Todorov 1981. See also PRATTON.

algebrization. The opposite of DEFAMILIARIZATION. Whereas the latter, for Shklovsky and the Russian Formalists, results from techniques (sets of devices) that make the familiar strange by impeding automatic, habitual ways of perceiving, algebrization overautomatizes perception and allows for the greatest economy of perceptive effort. ¶Lemon & Reis 1965; Shklovsky 1965a.

allomotif. A MOTIF occurring in a particular motifemic context; a motif manifesting a specific MOTIFEME. Given a situation in which it is forbidden to gather apples, for instance, a motif such as "The princess gathered apples" would be said to constitute an allomotif of the motifeme "violation." Allomotifs are to motifemes what allophones (variants of the same distinctive sound class) are to phonemes (distinctive sound classes) and allomorphs to morphemes. ¶Dundes 1964.

alteration. An isolated change in FOCALIZATION; a momentary infraction to the focalization code governing a narrative. There are two types of alteration: giving more information (PARALEPSIS) or giving less information (PARALIPSIS) than should be given in terms of the governing code. ¶Genette 1980.

alternation. A combination of narrative SEQUENCES (recounted in the same NARRATING INSTANCE or in different ones) such that units of one sequence are made to alternate with units of another sequence; an INTERWEAVING of sequences. A narrative like "John was happy, and Mary was unhappy; then John got divorced, and Mary got married; then John became unhappy, and Mary became happy" can be said to result from the alternation of one unit from "John was happy; then John got divorced; then John became unhappy" and one unit from "Mary was unhappy; then Mary got married; then Mary became happy." ¶Along with LINKING and EMBEDDING, alternation is one of the basic ways of combining narrative sequences. ¶Ducrot and Todorov 1979; Prince 1973, 1982; Todorov 1966, 1981. See also COMPLEX STORY.

amplitude. See EXTENT. ¶Chatman 1978.

anachrony. A discordance between the order in which events (are said to) occur and the order in which they are recounted: a beginning IN MEDIAS RES followed by a return to earlier events constitutes a typical example of anachrony. ¶In relation to the "present" moment, the moment when the chronological recounting of a sequence of events is interrupted to make room for them, anachronies can go back to the past (RETROSPECTION, ANALEPSIS, FLASHBACK) or forward to the future (ANTICIPATION, PROLEPSIS, FLASHFORWARD). They have a certain EXTENT or AMPLITUDE (they cover a certain amount of STORY TIME) as well as a certain REACH (the story time they cover is at a certain temporal distance from the "present" moment): in "Mary sat down. Four years later she would have the very same impression and her excitement would last for a whole month," the anachrony has an extent of one month and a reach of four years. ¶Bal 1985; Chatman 1978; Genette 1980; Mosher 1980. See also ORDER.

anagnorisis. See RECOGNITION. ¶Aristotle 1968.

analepsis. An ANACHRONY going back to the past with respect to the "present" moment; an evocation of one or more events that occurred before the "present" moment (or moment when the chronological recounting of a sequence of events is interrupted to make room for the analepsis); a RETROSPECTION; a FLASHBACK: "John became furious and, though he had vowed, many years before, never to lose his temper, he began to shout hysterically." ¶Analepses have a certain EXTENT as well as a certain REACH: in "Mary could not face it. Yet she had spent several hours preparing for it the day before," the analepsis has an extent of several hours and a reach of one day. ¶Completing analepses, or RETURNS, fill in earlier gaps resulting from ELLIPSES in the narrative. Repeating analepses, or RECALLS, tell anew already mentioned past events. ¶Genette 1980; Rimmon 1976. See also ORDER, PROLEPSIS.

analysis. A technique whereby the thought and impressions of a character are recounted by the narrator in his or her own name and language. ¶Genette 1980. See

5

also INTERNAL ANALYSIS, NARRATIZED DISCOURSE.

analytic author. An OMNISCIENT NARRATOR (*The Red and the Black, Vanity Fair*). ¶Brooks and Warren 1959.

anisochrony. A variation in narrative SPEED; an acceleration or a slowdown in TEMPO. The change from SCENE to SUMMARY or summary to scene constitutes an anisochrony. ¶Genette 1980. See also ISOCHRONY.

antagonist. The major opponent of the PROTAGONIST. A narrative articulated in terms of an interpersonal CONFLICT involves two major characters with opposite goals: the protagonist (or the HERO) and the antagonist, or enemy. ¶Frye 1957. See also ANTISUBJECT, COUNTERPLOT.

anterior narration. A NARRATION preceding in time the narrated situations and events; a PRIOR NARRATING. Anterior narration is characteristic of PREDICTIVE NARRATIVE. ¶Prince 1982.

anticipation. A PROLEPSIS, a FLASHFORWARD, an ANACHRONY going forward to the future with respect to the "present" moment (or moment when the chronological recounting of a sequence of events is interrupted to make room for the anticipation). ¶Chatman 1978; Genette 1980; Lämmert 1955; Prince 1982. See also ADVANCE NOTICE, ORDER.

anticlimax. An event or series of events (especially at the end of a narrative or narrative SEQUENCE) noticeably and surprisingly less important than the events leading up to it; an effect turning out to be strikingly less significant or intense than expected; a break in the progressive intensification of a series of events or effects. ¶Brooks and Warren 1959. See also CLIMAX.

antidonor. The opposite of the DONOR. The antidonor is a homologue of the OPPONENT. ¶Greimas and Courtés 1982.

antihero. An unheroic HERO; a hero defined by negative or less than admirable attributes; a PROTAGONIST whose characteristics are antithetical to those traditionally associated with a hero. Bardamu in Céline's *Journey to the End of the Night,* Jim Dixon in Kingsley Amis's *Lucky Jim,* and Yossarian in Heller's *Catch-22* are antiheroes. ¶Scholes and Kellogg 1966.

antinarrative. A (verbal or nonverbal) text adopting the trappings of narrative but systematically calling narrative logic and narrative conventions into question; an ANTISTORY. Robbe-Grillet's *Jealousy* and Beckett's *Molloy* are antinarratives. ¶Chatman 1978.

antisender. The opposite of the SENDER. The latter sends the SUBJECT on its quest and imparts a set of values to it; the Antisender represents an opposite set of values and sends the ANTISUBJECT on a quest that is at cross-purposes with that of the Subject. ¶Greimas and Courtés 1982; Hénault 1983.

antistory. See ANTINARRATIVE. ¶Chatman 1978.

antisubject. The opposite of the SUBJECT. The Antisubject has aims that are at cross-purposes with those of the Subject. It should not be viewed as a mere OPPONENT incidentally coming into conflict with or representing a momentary obstacle for the Subject in the latter's pursuit of its goal.

Like the latter, it is a quester, and the narrative is articulated in terms of their conflicting quests: in "The Final Problem," Holmes represents the Subject and Moriarty the Antisubject. ¶If the Subject is concretized as the PROTAGONIST at the level of narrative SURFACE STRUCTURE, the Antisubject is concretized as the ANTAGONIST. ¶Greimas and Courtés 1982; Hénault 1983; Rastier 1973. See also ANTISENDER.

appellative function. The CONACTIVE FUNCTION. ¶K. Bühler 1934. See also CONSTITUTIVE FACTORS OF COMMUNICATION, FUNCTIONS OF COMMUNICATION.

archipersona. An ACTANT; a fundamental narrative ROLE. ¶Lotman 1977.

argument 1. The summary of a narrative (usually consisting of the most important KERNELS making up that narrative). 2. In Aristotelian terms, the set of events significantly involved in the ACTION of a play or epic. Some of these events may lie outside the PLOT proper of the epic or play: they may occur before its BEGINNING, for example. In other words, argument is a larger concept than plot: the murder of Laius is part of the argument of *Oedipus Rex* but not part of its plot. ¶Aristotle 1968; Barthes 1975.

aspect. The VISION in terms of which a story is presented; FOCALIZATION; POINT OF VIEW. ¶Todorov 1966.

atomic story. A string of MOTIFS governed by modal homogeneity: all modal formulas in an atomic story are constructed with operators pertaining to one and only one modality. Atomic stories can be alethic (governed by operators of possibility, impossibility, and necessity), deontic (governed by operators of permission, prohibition, and obligation), axiological (governed by operators of goodness, badness, and indifference), and epistemic (governed by operators of knowledge, ignorance, and belief). Given a string of motifs analyzable as Lack (of some value)—Liquidation of Lack, for example, the string would constitute an axiological atomic story. ¶Doležel 1976. See also COMPOUND STORY, MODALITY, MOLECULAR STORY.

attempt. In STORY GRAMMARS, a character's effort to reach a GOAL or SUBGOAL. Attempts usually consist of one or more EVENTS or of an entire EPISODE. ¶Thorndyke 1977.

attribute. 1. A character TRAIT. 2. In Propp's terminology, an external (as opposed to functional) quality of a fairy-tale character, specifying his or her age, status, sex, appearance, etc. Two HEROES can have very different attributes (though they fulfill the same functions), and so can two DONORS or two VILLAINS. ¶Garvey 1978; Propp 1968.

attributive discourse. The discourse accompanying a character's (direct) discourse and specifying the act of the speaker or thinker, identifying him or her, and (sometimes) indicating various dimensions or features of the act, the character, the setting in which they appear, etc.: "—How are you? *inquired John in a sonorous voice while opening the door to the back room.*" Attributive discourse in a narrative is equivalent to the set of TAG CLAUSES in that narrative. ¶Prince 1978; Shapiro 1984.

auctorial narrative type. The class of HOMO-
DIEGETIC or HETERODIEGETIC NARRATIVES
characterized by ZERO FOCALIZATION *(Moby
Dick, Bella, Eugénie Grandet, Tom Jones).*
Along with the ACTORIAL and the NEUTRAL
NARRATIVE TYPES, it is one of three basic
classes in Lintvelt's typology. ¶Genette
1983; Lintvelt 1981. See also POINT OF
VIEW.

auktoriale Erzählsituation. See AUTHORIAL
NARRATIVE SITUATION. ¶Stanzel 1964, 1971,
1984.

Aussage. One of two linguistic subsystems,
according to Hamburger, who opposes it to
what she calls FIKTIONALE ERZÄHLEN (fictional recounting). *Aussage* (statement)
consists of historical, theoretical, and pragmatic reality statements (as well as
"feigned reality" statements occurring, for
example, in FIRST-PERSON NARRATIVE fiction): these are all relatable to a real (or
feigned) I-Origo, a real (or feigned) originary "I" and his or her subjectivity.
Fiktionale Erzählen, on the other hand,
consists of THIRD-PERSON NARRATIVE fiction.
It is characterized by the absence of an
I-Origo (fictive characters introduced as
third persons are the subjects of the utterances, thoughts, feelings, and actions
presented), and it has the unique ability to
portray the subjectivity of these third persons *qua* third persons. ¶Hamburger's
distinction between *Aussage* and *fiktionale
Erzählen* is analogous though by no means
equivalent to Benveniste's distinction between DISCOURS and HISTOIRE and Weinrich's distinction between BESPROCHENE
WELT and ERZÄHLTE WELT. ¶Banfield 1982;
Hamburger 1973.

authentication function. The function in
terms of which a given MOTIF or NARRATIVE
STATEMENT is authenticated (assigned the
status of a fact, given the value "authentic"
as opposed to "nonauthentic"). In THIRD-
PERSON NARRATIVE, for example, motifs introduced by the narrator's discourse are
(conventionally) taken to be authentic; on
the other hand, motifs introduced by the
characters' discourse are not: depending
on the narrator's declarations (and the
course of the action), they can turn out to
be authentic or nonauthentic. ¶Doležel
1980; Martínez-Bonati 1981; Ryan 1984.
See also NARRATIVE WORLD.

author. The maker or composer of a narrative. This real or concrete author is not to
be confused with the IMPLIED AUTHOR of a
narrative or with its NARRATOR and, unlike
them, is not immanent to or deducible from
the narrative. *Nausea* and "Erostratus," for
instance, have the same author—Sartre—
but different implied authors as well as different narrators. Similarly, a narrative can
have two or more real authors and one implied author or one narrator (*Naked Came
the Stranger,* the novels of Delly, Ellery
Queen, etc.). ¶Beardsley 1958; Booth
1983; Chatman 1978; Gibson 1950; Kayser
1958; Lintvelt 1981; Schmid 1973; Tillotson 1959.

authorial discourse. A narrative discourse
displaying signs of its NARRATOR or AUTHOR
and of his or her sovereign authority. As a
discursive mode, authorial (or auctorial)
discourse corresponds to the AUTHORIAL
NARRATIVE SITUATION. It is the discourse of
so-called OMNISCIENT NARRATORS and characterizes such novels as *Tom Jones,*

Fathers and Sons, and *Eugénie Grandet.*
¶Genette 1980.

authorial narrative situation. A NARRATIVE
SITUATION characterized by the omniscience
of a NARRATOR who is not a participant in
the situations and events recounted *(Tom
Jones, A Tale of Two Cities, Vanity Fair,
Eugénie Grandet).* Along with the FIRST-
PERSON and the FIGURAL NARRATIVE SITU-
ATIONS, the authorial narrative situation
(AUKTORIALE ERZÄHLSITUATION) is one of
three basic types in Stanzel's classification.
¶Stanzel 1964, 1971, 1984. See also AU-
THORIAL DISCOURSE, OMNISCIENT NARRATOR,
VISION, ZERO FOCALIZATION.

authority. The extent of a narrator's knowl-
edge of the narrative situations and events.
An OMNISCIENT NARRATOR *(Tom Jones, The
Red and the Black)* has more authority
than one who does not provide an INSIDE
VIEW of the characters ("Hills Like White El-
ephants"). ¶Chatman 1978. See also
PRIVILEGE.

author's intrusion. **1.** An intervention by
the NARRATOR in the form of a comment on
the situations and events presented, their
presentation or its context; a commentarial
excursus by the narrator (Blin): "I know
not, be it remarked by the way, whether
this is not the same cell, the interior of
which may still be seen through a small
square aperture on the east side, at about
the height of a man, on the platforms from
which the towers rise." **2.** In fiction, a
passage felt to engage the responsibility of
the AUTHOR as opposed to that of the narrator, a passage taken to betray the real
author's hand. ¶Banfield 1982; Blin 1954;
Genette 1980. See also COMMENTARY,

INTRUSIVE NARRATOR.

author's second self. See IMPLIED AUTHOR.
¶Tillotson 1959.

autodiegetic narrative. A FIRST-PERSON
NARRATIVE the NARRATOR of which is also
the PROTAGONIST or the HERO; a variety of
HOMODIEGETIC NARRATIVE such that the
narrator is also the main character *(Great
Expectations, Kiss Me Deadly, The
Stranger).* ¶Genette 1980; Lanser 1981.
See also DIEGETIC.

autonomous monologue. IMMEDIATE DIS-
COURSE *(Les Lauriers sont coupés).* As
opposed to the QUOTED MONOLOGUE, which
is introduced by a narrator, the autonomous monologue is free of all narratorial
mediation or patronage. ¶Cohn 1978,
1981. See also INTERIOR MONOLOGUE.

auxiliant. An ACTANTIAL ROLE whereby the
SUBJECT is qualified along the axis of ability
(modalized as being able or not being able
to do). At the SURFACE STRUCTURE level,
the auxiliant can be represented by the
same ACTOR as the one representing the
unmodalized Subject or by a different actor. When the latter obtains, and depending
on the positive or negative nature of the
auxiliant, the actor functions as a HELPER
or an OPPONENT. ¶Greimas and Courtés
1982. See also MODALITY.

B

background. The narrative space, SETTING,
or collection of EXISTENTS and EVENTS
against which other existents and events

9

emerge and come to the fore. ¶Chatman 1978; Liddell 1947; Weinrich 1964. See also FIGURE, FOREGROUND, GROUND.

balance. One of six fundamental ROLES isolated by Souriau in his study of the possibilities of drama. The Balance (analogous to Propp's DISPATCHER and Greimas's SENDER) is the arbiter or rewarder, the attributor of the good, the imparter of values. ¶Scholes 1974; Souriau 1950. See also ACTANT.

baring the device. See LAYING BARE. ¶Tomashevsky 1965.

beginning. The incident initiating the process of change in a PLOT or ACTION. This incident does not necessarily follow but is necessarily followed by other incidents. ¶Students of NARRATIVE have emphasized that the beginning, which corresponds to the passage from quiescence, homogeneity, and indifference to irritation, heterogeneity and difference, provides narrative with a forward-looking intention. It gives rise to a certain number of possibilities, and reading (processing) a narrative is, among other things, wondering which will and which will not be realized and finding out. ¶Aristotle 1968; Brooks 1984; Martin 1986; Prince 1982; Said 1975. See also END, MIDDLE, NARRATIVITY.

behaviorist narrative. An OBJECTIVE NARRATIVE; a narrative characterized by EXTERNAL FOCALIZATION and thus limited to the conveyance of the characters' behavior (words and actions but not thought or feelings), their appearance, and the setting against which they come to the fore ("The Killers"). ¶In this type of narrative, the narrator tells less than one or several characters know and abstains from direct commentary and interpretation. ¶N. Friedman 1955b; Genette 1980; Lintvelt 1981; Prince 1982; Romberg 1962; Souvage 1965. See also DRAMATIC MODE, NEUTRAL NARRATIVE TYPE, POINT OF VIEW, VISION.

besprochene Welt. According to Weinrich, one of two distinct and complementary categories of textual worlds, comprising such forms as dialogue, lyric poetry, the critical essay, the political memorandum, and the scientific report, and—in English—signaled by the use of the present, the present perfect, and the future. In the *besprochene Welt* (commented world) category—as opposed to the ERZÄHLTE WELT (narrated world) category—the ADDRESSER and ADDRESSEE are directly linked to and concerned by what is described. ¶Weinrich's distinction between *besprochene Welt* and *erzählte Welt* is analogous to Benveniste's distinction between DISCOURS and HISTOIRE and is related to Hamburger's distinction between AUSSAGE and FIKTIONALE ERZÄHLEN. ¶Ricoeur 1985; Weinrich 1964. See also TENSE.

block characterization. A (relatively) thorough (physical and psychological) description of a CHARACTER upon one of his or her first appearances, a set-piece presentation of a character's TRAITS. ¶Souvage 1965. See also CHARACTERIZATION.

bound motif. A CARDINAL FUNCTION; a NUCLEUS; a KERNEL. For Tomashevsky and the Russian Formalists, bound motifs (as opposed to FREE MOTIFS) are logically essential to the narrative action and cannot be eliminated without destroying its causal-chronological coherence. ¶Tomashevsky 1965. See also MOTIF.

camera. One of eight types of POINT OF VIEW according to Friedman, who regards it as the ultimate in narratorial exclusion and gives as an example of it the opening section of Isherwood's *Goodbye to Berlin:* "I am a camera with its shutter open, quite passive, recording, not thinking. Recording the man shaving at the window opposite and the woman in the kimono washing her hair. Someday, all this will have to be developed, carefully printed, fixed." The camera or CAMERA EYE (presumably) records, without ostensible organization or selection, whatever is before it. ¶N. Friedman 1955b.

camera eye. A technique whereby the situations and events conveyed (presumably) "just happen" before a neutral recorder and are transmitted by it (*U.S.A.* trilogy); CAMERA. ¶Chatman 1978; N. Friedman 1955b; Magny 1972.

cardinal function. A KERNEL; a NUCLEUS; a BOUND MOTIF. As opposed to CATALYSES, cardinal functions are logically essential to the narrative action and cannot be eliminated without destroying its causal-chronological coherence. ¶Barthes 1975. See also FUNCTION.

catalysis. A SATELLITE; a FREE MOTIF; a minor event in a plot. As opposed to CARDINAL FUNCTIONS, catalyses are not log-ically essential to the narrative action, and their elimination does not destroy its causal-chronological coherence: rather than constituting crucial nodes in the action, they fill in the narrative space between these nodes. ¶Barthes 1975. See also FUNCTION.

catastrophe. The precipitating final stage of a play; the scene bringing the dramatic conflict to an end. The term usually designates the unhappy DENOUEMENT of tragedy. ¶Freytag 1894. See also FREYTAG'S PYRAMID, PLOT.

causality. A relation of cause and effect between (sets of) situations and/or events. ¶Causality can be explicit ("Mary liked to read because she was smart") or implicit ("It was raining, and John got wet"). When implicit, it is inferrable on logical, necessary grounds ("All gamblers are sad. Susan was a gambler. She was sad") or on pragmatic, probabilistic grounds: if one event follows another event in time and is (plausibly) relatable to it, the second event is taken to be caused by the first unless the narrative specifies otherwise (compare "Jane insulted Nancy, and Nancy felt bad" with "Jane insulted Nancy, and Nancy felt bad, but it had nothing to do with Jane's behavior"; or "Peter ate an apple and got sick" with "Peter ate an apple and got sick, but his doctors determined that the sickness was not caused by the apple"). According to Barthes (following Aristotle), the confusion between consecutiveness and consequence, chronology and causality, constitutes perhaps the most powerful motor of NARRATIVITY: narrative would represent the systematic exploitation of the

POST HOC ERGO PROPTER HOC FALLACY, whereby what-comes-after-X is interpreted as what-is-caused-by-X. ¶Whether implicit or explicit, causal links may reflect a psychological order (for example, a character's actions are the cause or consequence of his personality or her state of mind), a philosophical order (every event exemplifies the theory of universal determinism, for instance), a social order, a political one, and so forth. ¶Aristotle 1968; Barthes 1975; Chatman 1978; Pratt 1977; Prince 1982; Todorov 1981. See also METONYMY, NARRATIVE, PLOT.

central consciousness. FOCALIZER; REFLECTOR; CENTRAL INTELLIGENCE; holder of POINT OF VIEW. The central consciousness is the consciousness through which situations and events are perceived. ¶H. James 1972. See also FOCALIZATION, FOCUS OF NARRATION, PERSPECTIVE.

central intelligence. See CENTRAL CONSCIOUSNESS. ¶H. James 1972.

character. **1.** An EXISTENT endowed with anthropomorphic traits and engaged in anthropomorphic actions; an ACTOR with anthropomorphic attributes. ¶Characters can be more or less major or minor (in terms of textual prominence), dynamic (when they change) or static (when they do not), consistent (when their attributes and actions do not result in contradiction) or inconsistent, and FLAT (simple, two-dimensional, endowed with very few traits, highly predictable in behavior) or ROUND (complex, multidimensional, capable of surprising behavior). They are also classable in terms of their actions, or their words, their feelings, their appearance, etc.; in terms of their conformity to standard ROLES (the *eiron* or self-deprecator, the *alazon* or braggart, the ingénue, the *femme fatale,* the cuckold) or TYPES; and in terms of their correspondence to certain SPHERES OF ACTION (that of the HERO or that of the VILLAIN, for instance) or their concretizing certain ACTANTS (the SENDER, the RECEIVER, the SUBJECT, the OBJECT). ¶Though the term *character* is most often used with reference to existents in the world of the situations and events recounted, it is also used sometimes to refer to the NARRATOR and the NARRATEE. **2.** An actor; an existent engaged in an action. **3.** In Aristotelian terms, and along with THOUGHT (DIANOIA), one of two qualities that an AGENT (or PRATTON) has. Character (ETHOS) is the element in accordance with which agents can be said to be of a certain type. It is a secondary element, consisting of the type traits added to the agent in order to characterize it. Whereas thought is revealed by the agent's statements as well as by his or her thinking and arguing, character is revealed by the agent's choices, decisions, and actions, and by the way they are performed. ¶Alexandrescu 1974; Aristotle 1968; Barthes 1974; Bourneuf and Ouellet 1975; Bremond 1973; Chatman 1978; Ducrot and Todorov 1979; Forster 1927; N. Friedman 1975; Frye 1957; Garvey 1978; Hamon 1972, 1983; Harvey 1965; Hochman 1985; Lotman 1977; Scholes and Kellogg 1966; Todorov 1969; Zeraffa 1969. See also ANTAGONIST, CHARACTERIZATION, PROTAGONIST, STOCK CHARACTER.

character-I. The "I" of a CHARACTER who also functions as the NARRATOR of the situations and events in which he or she plays a part. In "I ate a hamburger," the "I" who ate is the character-I and the "I" who tells about the eating the NARRATOR-I. ¶Prince 1982. See also FIRST-PERSON NARRATIVE, HOMODIEGETIC NARRATIVE.

characterization. **1.** The set of techniques resulting in the constitution of CHARACTER. Characterization can be more or less direct (a character's TRAITS are reliably stated by the narrator, the character herself, or another character) or indirect (deducible from the character's actions, reactions, thoughts, emotions, etc.); it can rely on a set-piece presentation of the character's (main) attributes (BLOCK CHARACTERIZATION) or favor their introduction one at a time; it can emphasize their permanence or underline their mutableness; it can privilege typicality (making the character conform to a certain TYPE) or, on the contrary, individualization; and so forth. **2.** In Aristotelian terms, the assignment of type traits to an AGENT (PRATTON). Characterization observes four principles: the agent should have a certain moral elevation *(chreston);* s/he should be endowed with traits appropriately related to the action *(harmotton);* s/he should have idiosyncrasies and be like an individual *(homoios);* and s/he should be consistent *(homalon).* ¶Aristotle 1968; Booth 1983; Chatman 1978; Ducrot and Todorov 1979; Garvey 1978; Hamon 1972, 1983; Lubbock 1921; Margolin 1983; Scholes and Kellogg 1966; Wellek and Warren 1949. See also EMBLEM, MASK, STOCK CHARACTER.

chronological order. The arrangement of situations and events in the order of their occurrence. "Harry washed, then he slept" observes chronological order, whereas "Harry slept after he worked" does not. ¶Chronological order is very much privileged by positivistic historiography. ¶Prince 1973. See also FABULA, ORDER, STORY.

chronotope. The nature of and relationship between represented temporal and spatial categories. The term designates and emphasizes the utter interdependence of space and time in (artistic) representations: it literally means "time-space." ¶Texts and classes of texts model reality and create world pictures according to different chronotopes (different kinds of time-space complexes) and are definable in terms of them. For example, the "adventure" chronotope, exemplified by such Greek romances as *Daphnis and Chloe* or *Aethiopica,* features a thoroughly abstract time (removed from historical and biographical times, consisting of unrelated and reversible moments, involving no biological or psychological transformation) that combines in an external manner with an equally nonspecific and nondetermining geographical space (the adventures depicted can occur in any number of locations and are in no way affected by them). ¶Bakhtin 1981; Clark and Holquist 1984.

classeme. In Greimassian terminology (adapted from Bernard Pottier's), a contextual SEME as opposed to a nuclear or basic one; a seme educed by the context in which it recurs. According to Greimas, the noun *roar,* for instance, which may be said to contain the nuclear seme "kind of cry," has the contextual seme "animal" in "the lion's roar was scary" and the contextual seme "human" in "the policeman's roar was scary." ¶Classemes provide texts with coherence. ¶Greimas 1983b; Greimas and Courtés 1982. See also ISOTOPY, SEMEME.

climax. The point of greatest tension; the culminating point in a progressive intensification. In traditional PLOT structure, the climax constitutes the highest point of the RISING ACTION. ¶Brooks and Warren 1959; Freytag 1894; Tomashevsky 1965. See also ANTICLIMAX, FALLING ACTION, FREYTAG'S PYRAMID.

coda. A statement indicating that a NARRATIVE is over: "and they lived happily ever after" is a common coda. ¶Labov 1972; Pratt 1977.

code. 1. One of the fundamental constituents of any act of (verbal) communication. The code is the system of norms, rules, and constraints in terms of which the MESSAGE signifies. It is at least partially common to the ADDRESSER and ADDRESSEE of the message. ¶The opposition between code and message is analogous to but more general than the famous Saussurean opposition between LANGUE (language system) and PAROLE (individual utterance): just as the language system governs the production (and reception) of the individual utterance, the code governs the production (and reception) of the message. **2.** One of the "voices" (models of the already-known, models of reality) out of which a narrative is woven. According to Barthes, narrative and its constitutive units signify in terms of one or more such voices or codes (PROAIRETIC, HERMENEUTIC, REFERENTIAL, SEMIC, SYMBOLIC, etc.). ¶Barthes 1974, 1981a; Culler 1975; Jakobson 1960; Mar-

tin 1986; Prince 1982. See also CONSTITUTIVE FACTORS OF COMMUNICATION, METALINGUAL FUNCTION, NARRATIVE CODE.

commentary. A commentarial excursus by the NARRATOR; an AUTHOR'S INTRUSION; a narratorial intervention going beyond the identification or description of EXISTENTS and the recounting of EVENTS. In commentary, the narrator explains the meaning or significance of a narrative element, makes value judgments, refers to worlds transcending the characters' world, and/or comments on his or her own narration. ¶Commentary can be simply ornamental; it can fulfill a rhetorical purpose; and it can function as an essential part of the dramatic structure of the narrative. ¶Booth 1983; Chatman 1978; Lintvelt 1981; Weinrich 1964. See also DESCRIPTION, DESCRIPTIVE PAUSE, DISCOURSE, EVALUATION, INTRUSIVE NARRATOR, NARRATION.

communication. See CONSTITUTIVE FACTORS OF COMMUNICATION.

competence. 1. See NARRATIVE COMPETENCE. **2.** In Greimassian terminology, that which makes action possible and, more specifically, the qualification of the SUBJECT along the axes of desire (wanting to do) and/or obligation (having to do) and the axes of knowledge (knowing how to do) and/or ability (being able to do). ¶Adam 1984, 1985; Greimas 1970, 1983a; Greimas and Courtés 1976, 1982; Hénault 1983; Prince 1981, 1981–82. See also MODALITY, NARRATIVE SCHEMA, PERFORMANCE.

complex story. A story combining two or more (MINIMAL) STORIES or NARRATIVES through LINKING, EMBEDDING, or ALTERNATION. "John was rich and Mary was poor;

then Mary won the lottery and she became rich; then John squandered his money and he became poor" represents a complex story that can be said to obtain from the embedding of "Mary was poor; then Mary won the lottery, and she became rich" into "John was rich; then John squandered his money, and he became poor." ¶Prince 1973. See also SEQUENCE.

complicating action. In Labov's terminology, the part of a NARRATIVE that defines it as such. The complicating action follows the ORIENTATION and leads to the RESULT or RESOLUTION. It is the MIDDLE of an ACTION, the COMPLICATION, the bridge between the initial situation and its final modification. If a narrative is taken to constitute a series of answers to certain questions, the complicating action is that constituent of it answering the question "Then what happened?" ¶Labov 1972; Pratt 1977.

complication. **1.** The part of a narrative following the EXPOSITION and leading to the DENOUEMENT; the MIDDLE of an ACTION; the COMPLICATING ACTION; the RAVELLING. **2.** In traditional PLOT structure, the RISING ACTION (from EXPOSITION to CLIMAX). **3.** In Proppian terms, FUNCTIONS VIII–XI: villainy or lack, mediation, beginning counteraction, and departure. **4.** In Aristotelian terms, the situation obtaining before the BEGINNING of the action; *desis.* ¶Aristotle 1968; Brooks and Warren 1959; Freytag 1894; Propp 1968. See also FREYTAG'S PYRAMID.

composition. See MOTIVATION. ¶Wellek and Warren 1949.

compound story. A story composed of two or more ATOMIC STORIES (two or more strings of MOTIFS governed by a different MODALITY); a MOLECULAR STORY. ¶Doležel 1976.

conative function. One of the FUNCTIONS OF COMMUNICATION in terms of which any communicative (verbal) act may be structured and oriented; the APPELLATIVE FUNCTION. When the communicative act is centered on the ADDRESSEE (rather than on one of the other CONSTITUTIVE FACTORS OF COMMUNICATION), it (mainly) has a conative function. More specifically, those passages in narrative focusing on the NARRATEE can be said to fulfill a conative function: "You will do the same, you, my reader, now holding this book in your white hands, and saying to yourself in the depths of your easy chair: I wonder if it will amuse me!" ¶Jakobson 1960; Prince 1982.

conceptual point of view. The world view or conceptual system in terms of which a situation or event is considered. ¶Chatman 1978. See also PERCEPTUAL POINT OF VIEW, POINT OF VIEW.

conflict. The struggle in which the ACTORS are engaged. The latter can fight against Fate or destiny, against their social or physical environment, or against one another (external conflict), and they can fight against themselves (internal or inner conflict). ¶Brooks and Warren 1959. See also NARRATIVITY.

conjoining. See LINKING.

conjunction. Along with DISJUNCTION, one of the two basic types of JUNCTION, or relation, between the SUBJECT and the OBJECT ("X is with Y," "X has Y"). ¶Greimas and Courtés 1982; Hénault 1983.

consonance. The fusion between a NARRA-

TOR and the character's consciousness he or she narrates *(Portrait of the Artist as a Young Man)*. Consonance is characteristic of the relationship between narrator and PROTAGONIST in a FIGURAL NARRATIVE SITUATION. ¶Cohn 1978. See also DISSONANCE.

constative. An utterance that reports events or states of affairs in certain worlds and therefore has the property of being "either true or false" in these worlds: "Napoleon won the battle of Austerlitz" and "The earth is flat" are constatives. ¶The theory of SPEECH ACTS originates in J. L. Austin's distinction between constatives and PERFORMATIVES (utterances like "I promise to come tomorrow" that are used to do rather than to say something, to perform an act rather than to state that something is or is not the case). However, as Austin goes on to argue, constatives are themselves performatives, since saying (asserting, stating, reporting) that something is or is not the case constitutes a kind of doing. ¶If narrative can be said to "constate," to report that certain situations and events are the case in certain worlds, it can also be said to perform (at the very least) the act of reporting. ¶Austin 1962; Lyons 1977; Pratt 1977. See also ILLOCUTIONARY ACT.

constitutional model. See CONSTITUTIVE MODEL.

constitutive factors of communication. The elements entering into any act of (verbal) communication and essential to its operation. ¶Bühler had isolated three such elements: the ADDRESSER, the ADDRESSEE, and the CONTEXT. Jakobson, in what has proven to be the most influential model of communication in NARRATOLOGY, proposed a six-factor schema including the addresser (the sender or encoder of the MESSAGE), the addressee (the receiver or decoder of the message), the message itself, the CODE (in terms of which the message signifies), the context (or REFERENT to which the message refers), and the CONTACT (the psychophysiological connection between the addresser and the addressee):

Context

Message

Addresser-- Addressee

Contact

Code

Some theorists (Hymes, for example) prefer to speak of seven factors and replace context with topic (what is communicated about) and setting (the scene, the situation, the context of the communicative act). ¶To each of the factors corresponds a particular FUNCTION OF COMMUNICATION, and any communicative act fulfills one or more of these functions. ¶K. Bühler 1934; Hymes 1970; Jakobson 1960.

constitutive model. The Greimassian model describing the elementary structure of signification, the model accounting for the basic articulations of meaning within a semantic micro-universe. It is represented visually by the SEMIOTIC SQUARE. ¶Greimas 1970, 1983b; Greimas and Courtés 1982.

contact. 1. One of the fundamental constituents of any act of (verbal) communication. The contact is the physical channel and psychological connection that allows the ADDRESSER and the ADDRESSEE to enter and stay in communication. **2.** The relation between the NARRATOR and the NARRATEE (Lanser). Along with STANCE and STATUS, contact is one of three basic relations in terms of which POINT OF VIEW is structured. ¶Jakobson 1960; Lanser 1981. See also CONSTITUTIVE FACTORS OF COMMUNICATION, PHATIC FUNCTION.

content. Following Hjelmslev, one of the two planes of any semiotic system: the "what" that is signified as opposed to the "way" it is signified. Like the EXPRESSION plane, the content plane has a FORM and a SUBSTANCE. ¶When used in connection with narrative, content can be said to be equivalent to STORY (as opposed to DISCOURSE). ¶Chatman 1978; Hjelmslev 1954, 1961; Prince 1973.

context. One of the fundamental constituents of any act of (verbal) communication. The context or REFERENT is that which the MESSAGE refers to, that which it is about. ¶Jakobson 1960. See also CONSTITUTIVE FACTORS OF COMMUNICATION, REFERENTIAL FUNCTION.

contract. **1.** See NARRATIVE CONTRACT. **2.** In the Greimassian model, an agreement between the SENDER and the SUBJECT. It provides the latter with a program to realize and can thus be said to constitute the mainspring of (canonical) NARRATIVES. ¶The Subject can fulfill (or fail to fulfill) the contract and be rewarded (or punished). ¶Adam 1984; Barthes 1974; Greimas 1983a, 1983b; Greimas and Courtés 1982. See also MANIPULATION, SANCTION.

coordinate clauses. Clauses having identical DISPLACEMENT SETS. In "The birds kept on singing. The bells kept on ringing. John suddenly got up and went into the bedroom," the first two sentences are coordinate clauses. ¶Labov and Waletzky 1967. See also FREE CLAUSE, NARRATIVE CLAUSE, RESTRICTED CLAUSE.

counterplot. A unified set of actions directed toward a result opposite the result intended by the actions of the (main) PLOT: the ANTAGONIST'S actions and goals can be taken to make up a counterplot. ¶Souvage 1965.

covert narrator. An effaced NARRATOR; a non-INTRUSIVE and UNDRAMATIZED NARRATOR; a narrator presenting situations and events with a minimum amount of narratorial mediation ("The Dead," *The Spoils of Poynton*). Covert narrators are typical of positivistic historiography. ¶Chatman 1978. See also ABSENT NARRATOR, DRAMATIZED NARRATOR, OVERT NARRATOR.

crisis. The TURNING POINT, the decisive moment on which the plot will turn. ¶Holman 1972; Madden 1979.

cultural code. The REFERENTIAL CODE. ¶All of the codes or models of the already-known are culturally determined; but the so-called referential or cultural code is the most obviously cultural among them. ¶Barthes 1974; 1981a.

cutback. An ANALEPSIS, a FLASHBACK, a RETROSPECTION, a SWITCHBACK. ¶Brooks and Warren 1959. See also ORDER.

D

decisive test. One of the three TESTS characterizing the movement of the SUBJECT in the canonical NARRATIVE SCHEMA. Presupposed by the GLORIFYING TEST and presupposing the QUALIFYING TEST, the decisive (or main) test results in the CONJUNCTION of Subject and OBJECT. ¶Greimas 1983a, 1983b; Greimas and Courtés 1982; Hénault 1983. See also PERFORMANCE.

deep structure. The abstract underlying structure of narrative; the MACROSTRUCTURE of narrative. The deep structure consists of global syntactico-semantic representations determining the meaning of the narrative and is converted into SURFACE STRUCTURE by a set of operations or of TRANSFORMATIONS. In the Greimassian model of narrative, for example, whereas ACTANTS and actantial relations would be elements of the deep structure, ACTORS and actorial relations would be found at the surface-structure level. In other models of narrative, whereas the deep structure might be said to correspond to STORY, the surface structure might be said to correspond to DISCOURSE. ¶The term and concept were adapted from Chomsky and generative-transformational grammar. ¶Chomsky 1965; van Dijk 1972; Füger 1972; Johnson and Mandler 1980. See also NARRATIVE GRAMMAR.

defamiliarization. Making the familiar strange by impeding automatic, habitual ways of perceiving. For Shklovsky and the Russian Formalists, defamiliarization (OS-

TRANENIYE) captures the purpose of (literary) art: the promotion of awareness. ¶Lemon and Reis 1965; Shklovsky 1965a. See also ALGEBRIZATION.

deictic. Any term or expression which, in an utterance, refers to the context of production (ADDRESSER, ADDRESSEE, time, place) of that utterance: "here," "now," "yesterday," "I," "you," etc., are deictics, and in a statement like "She saw him yesterday," the adverb helps to locate what is reported relative to the addresser (in terms of his or her present, what is reported occurred the day before). ¶Käte Hamburger noted that, in narrative fiction, deictic (temporal) adverbials—which, in statements about reality, refer in terms of a present—are often linked to past tenses: consider "Mary learned that John was in town. She *now* faced a crucial decision" or "He got angry. *Yesterday,* he had accepted everything, but he wasn't going to take it anymore." She interpreted this as evidence that, rather than signifying real time, rather than labelling the situations and events narrated as pertaining to a former time, past tenses in narrative fiction designate these situations and events as fictive and as "occurring" in the characters' fictive and "time-less" present. ¶Benveniste 1971; Hamburger 1973; Palmer 1981. See also DEIXIS, EPIC PRETERITE, SHIFTER, TENSE.

deixis. The general phenomenon of the occurrence of DEICTICS; the set of references to the situation (interlocutors, time, place) of an utterance. ¶Benveniste 1971; Palmer 1981.

denouement. The outcome or untying of the PLOT; the UNRAVELLING of the COMPLICA-

TION; the END. ¶Ejxenbaum 1971a. See also CATASTROPHE, FALLING ACTION, RESOLUTION.

description. The representation of objects, beings, situations, or (nonpurposeful, nonvolitional) happenings in their spatial rather than temporal existence, their topological rather than chronological functioning, their simultaneity rather than succession. It is traditionally distinguished from NARRATION and from COMMENTARY. ¶Any description can be said to consist of a theme designating the object, being, situation, or happening described (e.g., "house") and a set of subthemes designating its component parts (e.g., "door," "room," "window," "wall"). The theme or subthemes can be characterized qualitatively (in terms of their qualities: "the door was beautiful," "the wall was green") or functionally (in terms of their function or use: "the room was only used for special occasions"). ¶A description can be more or less detailed and precise; objective or subjective; typical and stylized or, on the contrary, individualizing; decorative or explanatory/functional (establishing the tone or mood of a passage, conveying plot-relevant information, contributing to characterization, introducing or reinforcing a theme, symbolizing a conflict to come); and so on and so forth. ¶Bal 1977, 1983, 1985; Bonheim 1982, Bourneuf and Ouellet 1975; Debray-Genette 1980, 1982; Genette 1976, 1983; Hamon 1981, 1982; Ricardou 1967, 1971, 1973, 1978; Riffaterre 1972, 1972–73. See also DESCRIPTIVE PAUSE, SET DESCRIPTION, SETTING.

descriptive pause. A PAUSE occasioned by a DESCRIPTION. ¶Not all pauses are descriptive pauses: some are the result of COMMENTARY. Furthermore, not every description occasions a pause in the narrative: "The hall . . . was rather shallow in proportion to its length, and opened in great arched bays into a sort of lobby surrounding it, in which serving-tables were placed" constitutes a descriptive pause because it does not correspond to any passage of time in the world represented (by *The Magic Mountain*). On the other hand, "After the fish followed an excellent meat dish, with garnishings, then a separate vegetable course, then roast fowl, a pudding . . . and lastly cheese and fruit" does not constitute a descriptive pause (in the same narrative). ¶Genette 1980.

determination. The temporal limits of an ITERATIVE NARRATIVE; the span of time in which an event (or a set of events) is said to recur: "I went to summer camp every year, from 1959 to 1964" has a determination of five years. ¶Genette 1980.

diachronic analysis. The study of changes in (linguistic) systems or parts thereof across time. ¶Saussure 1966. See also SYNCHRONIC ANALYSIS.

dialogic narrative. A narrative characterized by the interaction of several voices, consciousnesses, or world views, none of which unifies or is superior to (has more authority than) the others; a POLYPHONIC NARRATIVE. In dialogic as opposed to MONOLOGIC NARRATIVE, the narrator's views, judgments, and even knowledge do not constitute the ultimate authority with respect to the world represented but only one contribution among several, a contribution that is in dialogue with and frequently less significant and perceptive than that of (some of) the characters. According to Bakhtin, Dostoevsky's fiction (say, *The Brothers Karamazov*) provides particularly good examples of dialogic narrative. ¶Bakhtin 1981, 1984; Pascal 1977.

dialogue. The representation (dramatic in type) of an oral exchange involving two or more characters. In dialogue, the characters' speeches are presented as they (supposedly) were uttered and may or may not be accompanied by TAG CLAUSES. ¶Głowiński 1974; Stanzel 1984. See also ABRUPTIVE DIALOGUE, DIRECT SPEECH, MONOLOGUE, REPORTED SPEECH, SCENE.

dianoia. See THOUGHT. ¶Aristotle 1968.

diegesis. 1. The (fictional) world in which the situations and events narrated occur (in French, *diégèse*). 2. TELLING, recounting, as opposed to SHOWING, enacting (in French; *diégésis*). ¶Aristotle 1968; Genette 1980, 1983; Plato 1968. See also DIEGETIC, MIMESIS.

diegetic. Pertaining to or part of a given DIEGESIS *(diégèse)* and, more particularly, that diegesis represented by the (PRIMARY) NARRATIVE. ¶Narratives, narrators and narratees, existents and events, are characterizable in diegetic terms. Existents, for example, can be part of different diegeses, or they can belong to the same one (they are then said to be ISODIEGETIC). Similarly, narrators can be described according to DIEGETIC LEVEL. They can be EXTRADIEGETIC (not part of, external to, any diegesis); they can be DIEGETIC or INTRADIEGETIC (belonging to the diegesis presented in a primary narrative by an ex-

tradiegetic narrator); and they can appear in a METADIEGETIC or HYPODIEGETIC NARRATIVE (a narrative embedded within the diegetic or intradiegetic narrative). Furthermore, narrators can also be characterized in terms of the role (or lack thereof) they play in the diegesis they present: a HOMODIEGETIC NARRATOR is one who is a character in the situations and events s/he recounts (when s/he is the protagonist of these situations and events, an AUTODIEGETIC NARRATIVE obtains); a HETERODIEGETIC NARRATOR, on the other hand, is one who is not a character in the situations and events s/he recounts. Finally, when a SECOND-DEGREE NARRATIVE is brought up to the level of the primary narrative (when a metadiegetic narrative functions as if it were a diegetic one), a PSEUDO-DIEGETIC or REDUCED METADIEGETIC NARRATIVE obtains. ¶Genette 1980, 1983; Rimmon 1976.

diegetic level. The level at which an existent, event, or act of recounting is situated with regard to a given DIEGESIS *(diégèse).* In *Manon Lescaut,* for example, M. de Renoncourt's recounting of his memoirs occurs at an EXTRADIEGETIC level; the situations and events recounted in these memoirs (including Des Grieux's telling of his and Manon's adventures) occur at the DIEGETIC or INTRADIEGETIC level; and these adventures take place in a METADIEGETIC or HYPODIEGETIC NARRATIVE. ¶Genette 1980, 1983.

direct discourse. A TYPE OF DISCOURSE whereby a character's utterances or thoughts are given or quoted in the way the character (presumably) formulated them, as opposed to INDIRECT DISCOURSE:

compare "John said: —I am doing it" and "John said that he was doing it." In TAGGED DIRECT DISCOURSE, these formulations are accompanied by TAG CLAUSES characterizing some of their qualities, identifying the speaker (or thinker), etc.: "—It's the larynx, isn't it? Hans Castorp asked, inclining his head in answer"; "—And what kind of emissary are you, may I ask? Hans Castorp thought. Aloud he said: —Thank you, Professor Naphta." Sometimes, the formulations are not accompanied by a tag clause, but narratorial mediation is indicated by such signs as quotation marks, dashes, etc.: "—How are you? —Very well! and you?" In FREE DIRECT DISCOURSE, no tag clause is used and neither are other signs of narratorial mediation. ¶Chatman 1978; Genette 1980, 1983; Lanser 1981; Todorov 1981. See also REPORTED DISCOURSE.

direct speech. DIRECT DISCOURSE, especially direct discourse whereby a character's utterances (as opposed to thoughts) are represented. ¶Chatman 1978. See also DIALOGUE.

direct style. See DIRECT DISCOURSE.

discours. See DISCOURSE. ¶Benveniste 1971.

discourse. 1. The EXPRESSION plane of NARRATIVE as opposed to its CONTENT plane or STORY; the "how" of a narrative as opposed to its "what"; the NARRATING as opposed to the NARRATED; the NARRATION as opposed to the FICTION (in Ricardou's sense of the terms). ¶Discourse has a SUBSTANCE (a medium of MANIFESTATION: oral or written language, still or moving pictures, gestures, etc.) and a FORM (it consists of a connected set of NARRATIVE STATEMENTS that state the story and, more specifically, determine the ORDER of presentation of situations and events, the POINT OF VIEW governing that presentation, the narrative SPEED, the kind of COMMENTARY, and so on). "The man ate, then he slept" and "The man slept after he ate" have the same discourse substance (the written English language) but different discourse forms. 2. According to Benveniste, and along with history or story (HISTOIRE), one of two distinct and complementary linguistic subsystems. In discourse (DISCOURS), a link is established between a state or event and the situation in which that state or event is linguistically evoked. *Discours* thus involves some reference to the ENUNCIATION and implies a SENDER and a RECEIVER. *Histoire,* on the other hand, does not. Compare "He has gone" or "I've told you about it hundreds of times" with "He went" or "She told her about it hundreds of times." ¶Benveniste's distinction between *histoire* and *discours* is analogous to Weinrich's distinction between ERZÄHLTE WELT and BESPROCHENE WELT and reminiscent of Hamburger's distinction between FIKTIONALE ERZÄHLEN and AUSSAGE. ¶Benveniste 1971; Chatman 1978; Genette 1976, 1980, 1983. See also TENSE.

discourse time. The time taken by the representation of the NARRATED; the time of the NARRATING; ERZÄHLZEIT. ¶Chatman 1978. See also DURATION, STORY TIME, TENSE.

discovery. See RECOGNITION. ¶Aristotle 1968.

disjunction. Along with CONJUNCTION, one of two basic types of JUNCTION, or relation, between the SUBJECT and the OBJECT ("X is not with Y," "X does not have Y"). ¶Greimas and Courtés 1982; Hénault 1983.

dispatcher. One of the seven fundamental ROLES that a character may assume (in a fairy tale), according to Propp. The dispatcher (analogous to Greimas's SENDER and Souriau's BALANCE) sends the HERO off on his adventures. ¶Propp 1968. See also ACTANT, DRAMATIS PERSONA, SPHERE OF ACTION.

displacement set. The set consisting of (1) a given clause *c* in a sequence and (2) the clauses before and after which *c* can be placed in that sequence without altering the semantic interpretation. In "John went to greet the couple. The man stopped talking and the woman started to smile. John decided they were nice," the displacement set of "The man stopped talking" is "The man stopped talking and the woman started to smile." ¶Labov and Waletzky 1967. See also COORDINATE CLAUSES, FREE CLAUSE, NARRATIVE CLAUSE, RESTRICTED CLAUSE.

dissonance. The narrator's distancing of the character's consciousness he or she narrates ("Death in Venice"). Dissonance is characteristic of the relationship between NARRATOR and PROTAGONIST in an AUTHORIAL NARRATIVE SITUATION. ¶Cohn 1978. See also CONSONANCE, DISTANCE.

distance. **1.** Along with PERSPECTIVE, one of two major factors regulating narrative information (Genette). The more covert the narratorial mediation and the more numerous the details provided about the narrated situations and events, the smaller the distance that is said to obtain between them and their NARRATION. MIMESIS or SHOWING, for example, is taken to institute less distance than DIEGESIS or TELLING. **2.** The (metaphorical) space between NARRATOR, CHARACTERS, situations and events narrated, and NARRATEE. The distance can be temporal (I narrate events that happened two hours or two years ago); it can be intellectual (the narrator of *The Sound and the Fury* is far more intelligent than Benjy), moral (Sade's Justine is certainly more virtuous than the characters in her story), emotional (the narrator of "A Simple Heart" is not as moved by Virginie's death as Félicité is), and so on. Furthermore, a given distance can vary in the course of a narrative: at the end of *Tom Jones* the narrator and the narratee are emotionally closer than at the beginning. ¶Booth 1961, 1983; Genette 1980, 1983; Prince 1980, 1982. See also COVERT NARRATOR, MODE, MOOD, TONE.

donor. One of the seven fundamental ROLES that a character may assume (in a fairy tale), according to Propp. The donor (analogous to Greimas's HELPER and Souriau's MOON) provides the HERO with some agent (usually magical) that allows for the eventual liquidation of misfortune. ¶Propp 1968. See also ACTANT, ANTIDONOR, DRAMATIS PERSONA, SPHERE OF ACTION.

double focalization. The concurrence of two different FOCALIZATIONS in the rendering of a particular situation or event. ¶Double focalization is not infrequently used in film: in *Suspicion,* for example, when Lina reads the telegram Johnnie sent to tell her that he is going to attend the Hunt Ball, the end of the reading is shot so as to reflect both her own POINT OF VIEW and the more "objective" point of view of the camera. ¶Genette 1980.

double logic of narrative. The two organizing principles in terms of which (many a) NARRATIVE deploys itself, according to some narratologists. One principle emphasizes the primacy of event over meaning (insists upon event as the origin of meaning); the other stresses the primacy of meaning and its requirements (insists upon event as the effect of a will to meaning). The first principle emphasizes the (logical) priority of FABULA rather than SJUŽET; the second stresses the reverse (and makes *fabula* the product of *sjužet*). Each principle functions through the exclusion of the other, but paradoxically, both are necessary to the deployment of (many a) narrative, and the contradictory tension between them constitutes an important motor of narrative force or NARRATIVITY. ¶Brooks 1984; Culler 1981.

double plot. A PLOT involving two concurrent ACTIONS of (more or less) equal importance. ¶Empson 1960. See also COUNTERPLOT, SUBPLOT.

double vision. See DOUBLE FOCALIZATION. ¶Rogers 1965.

drama. SCENE; scenic rendering of speech (or thought) and behavior. The distinction made by James and Lubbock between drama and PANORAMA is analogous to the distinction between scene and SUMMARY or SHOWING and TELLING. ¶H. James 1972; Lubbock 1965. See also PICTURE.

dramatic mode. One of eight possible POINTS OF VIEW according to Friedman's classification. When the dramatic mode is adopted—as in the so-called OBJECTIVE or BEHAVIORIST NARRATIVE ("Hills Like White Elephants," *The Awkward Age*)—the information provided is largely limited to what the characters do and say, and there is no direct indication of what they perceive, think, or feel. ¶N. Friedman 1955b. See also EXTERNAL FOCALIZATION, EXTERNAL POINT OF VIEW.

dramatic monologue. INTERIOR MONOLOGUE. In dramatic monologue, the character's inner life is presented directly, without narratorial mediation. ¶The dramatic or interior monologue in narrative should be distinguished from the dramatic monologues composed by a Browning or a Tennyson: the latter are addressed to a possible interlocutor and have speech rather than thought as their formal base. ¶Banfield 1982; Scholes and Kellogg 1966.

dramatic treatment. In Jamesian terminology, the scenic rendering of situations and events and, more particularly, of the characters' speech and behavior. ¶H. James 1972. See also DRAMA, PANORAMA, PICTORIAL TREATMENT.

dramatis persona. In Proppian terminology, a fundamental ROLE (in a fairy tale) assumable by a character. Propp isolated seven such roles, each corresponding to a particular SPHERE OF ACTION: the VILLAIN, the DONOR (provider), the HELPER, the princess (a SOUGHT-FOR PERSON) and her father, the DISPATCHER, the HERO (seeker or victim), and the FALSE HERO. ¶Propp 1968. See also ACTANT.

dramatized narrator. A NARRATOR characterized in more or less detail as an "I." Though a dramatized narrator can be relatively effaced *(Madame Bovary),* it is more often provided with numerous physical, mental, and/or moral attributes *(Tom Jones).* In fact, it is frequently represented at the level of characters (in FIRST-PERSON or HOMODIEGETIC NARRATIVE) as a mere observer or witness ("A Rose for Emily"), a minor participant in the action *(A Study in Scarlet),* a relatively important participant *(The Great Gatsby),* or a protagonist *(The Confessions of Zeno, Great Expectations, Kiss Me Deadly).* ¶Booth 1983. See also COVERT NARRATOR, OVERT NARRATOR, UN-DRAMATIZED NARRATOR.

dual-voice hypothesis. The hypothesis according to which FREE INDIRECT DISCOURSE results from the mixing of two voices or language situations—that of a narrator and that of a character. ¶Pascal 1977.

Du-Form. SECOND-PERSON NARRATIVE form (you-form). ¶Füger 1972. See also ICH-FORM, ER-FORM.

duplication. The repetition, at the level of the NARRATED, of one or more (sequences of) events: "Joan attempted to climb the mountain and failed. She tried a second time and succeeded." ¶Suleiman 1980. See also TRIPLICATION.

duration. The set of phenomena pertaining to the relation between STORY TIME and DISCOURSE TIME. The former can be greater than the latter, equal to it, or smaller than it. ¶Duration is a problematic notion, particularly in the case of written narrative. Even if story time is specified (this event lasted ten minutes and that one twenty), discourse time (the time taken by the representation of story time) is difficult, not to say impossible, to measure: it is not equivalent to the (variable) time it takes to read or write a narrative nor is it the same as the time a given narration is said to have taken (imagine a three-page narration ending with "I started my account at nine o'clock and it is now twelve," or a three-hundred-page narration ending with the same sentence). This has led many narratologists to consider the study of SPEED or TEMPO preferable to (more fruitful than) that of duration. ¶Chatman 1978; Genette 1980; Metz 1974; Prince 1982. See also PACE, RHYTHM.

earth. One of six fundamental ROLES or FUNCTIONS isolated by Souriau (in his study of the possibilities of drama). The Earth (analogous to Greimas's RECEIVER) stands to benefit from the work of the LION. ¶Scholes 1974; Souriau 1950. See also ACTANT.

editorial omniscience. One of eight possible POINTS OF VIEW according to Friedman's classification: editorial omniscience characterizes the heterodiegetic, omniscient, and INTRUSIVE NARRATOR *(War and Peace).* ¶N. Friedman 1955b. See also HETERODIEGETIC NARRATOR, NEUTRAL OMNI-SCIENCE, OMNISCIENT POINT OF VIEW.

effet de réel. See REALITY EFFECT. ¶Barthes 1982.

ellipsis. A canonical narrative TEMPO; along with PAUSE, SCENE, STRETCH, and SUMMARY, one of the fundamental narrative SPEEDS. When there is no part of the narrative (no words or sentences, for example) corresponding to (representing) narratively pertinent situations and events that took time, ellipsis obtains. ¶An ellipsis can be frontal and merely institute a break in the temporal continuity (by skipping over one or several events, one or several moments of time), or it can be lateral (PARALIPSIS): in that case, it is not an intervening event that goes unmentioned but, rather, one or more components in a situation that is being recounted. In other words, given a series of events e_1, e_2, e_3 . . . e_n occurring at times t_1, t_2, t_3 . . . t_n, respectively or taking place at time t, we speak of ellipsis when one of the events is not mentioned. An ellipsis can also be explicit (underlined by the narrator, as in "I will not say anything about what happened during that fateful week") or implicit (inferable from a lacuna in the chronology or a break in the sequence of events recounted). ¶Chatman 1978; Genette 1980, Prince 1982.

embedded narrative. A narrative within a narrative; a METADIEGETIC NARRATIVE. ¶Genette 1980. See also EMBEDDING, FRAME NARRATIVE.

embedding. A combination of narrative SEQUENCES (recounted in the same NARRATING INSTANCE or in different ones) such that one sequence is embedded (set within) another one. A narrative like "Jane was happy, and Susan was unhappy; then Susan met Flora, and she became happy; then Jane met Peter, and she became unhappy" can be said to result from the embedding of "Susan was unhappy; then Susan met Flora, and she became happy" into "Jane was happy; then Jane met Peter, and she became unhappy." Similarly, *Manon Lescaut* can be said to result from the embedding of Des Grieux's narrative into the one recounted by M. de Renoncourt. ¶Along with LINKING and ALTERNATION, embedding (or NESTING) is one of the basic ways of combining narrative sequences. ¶Bal 1981b; Berendsen 1981; Bremond 1973; Ducrot and Todorov 1979; Prince 1973, 1982; Todorov 1966, 1981. See also METADIEGETIC NARRATIVE.

emblem. A CHARACTERIZATION device whereby a particular element in the world represented is evoked with each mention of a given CHARACTER and thus becomes distinctive of the latter. ¶Ducrot and Todorov 1979.

emic approach. An internal and functional (as opposed to an ETIC or external and taxonomic) approach to the study of (human) situations and productions. The emic approach defines and describes the constituents of a system in terms of the position and function attributed to them in it by its users. ¶Kenneth Pike coined the term *emic* by analogy with the term *phonemic*." ¶Dundes 1962, 1964; Pike 1967. See also ETIC APPROACH.

emotive function. One of the FUNCTIONS OF COMMUNICATION in terms of which any communicative (verbal) act may be structured and oriented; the EXPRESSIVE FUNCTION. When the communicative act is centered on the ADDRESSER (rather than on one of

the other CONSTITUTIVE FACTORS OF COMMU-
NICATION), it (mainly) has an emotive
function. More specifically, those passages
in narrative focusing on the NARRATOR can
be said to fulfill an emotive function: "I
really hate to evoke the events that happened then." ¶Jakobson 1960; Prince
1982.

enchainment. A mode of combining TRIADS
such that the outcome of one constitutes
the opening situation of another one. A
narrative like "He was happy; then he met
Peter; then he became unhappy; then he
met Paul; then he became happy" can be
said to result from the enchainment of "He
was happy; then he met Peter; then he became unhappy" and "He became unhappy;
then he met Paul; then he became happy."
¶Bremond 1973, 1980. See also LINKING.

end. The final incident in a PLOT or ACTION.
The end follows but is not followed by
other incidents and ushers a state of (relative) stability. ¶Students of NARRATIVE have
pointed out that the end occupies a deter-
minative position because of the light it
sheds (or might shed) on the meaning of
the events leading up to it. The end functions as the (partial) condition, the
magnetizing force, the organizing principle
of narrative: reading (processing) a narrative is, among other things, waiting for the
end, and the nature of the waiting is related to the nature of the narrative.
¶Aristotle 1968; Benjamin 1969; Brooks
1984; Genette 1968; Kermode 1967; Martin 1986; Prince 1982; Ricoeur 1985. See
also BEGINNING, MIDDLE, NARRATIVITY.

enunciatee. An ADDRESSEE. Should someone tell me a story, I am its enunciatee.

Should he or she tell the same story to
someone else, the latter is its enunciatee.
¶Greimas and Courtés 1976, 1982.

enunciation. **1.** The traces in a discourse
of the act (and its contextual dimensions)
generating that discourse. In "I will now recount a beautiful story," the DEICTICS "I"
and "now" are signs of the enunciation. **2.** The act (and its contextual
dimensions) generating a discourse. ¶Ben-
veniste 1971, 1974; Ducrot and Todorov
1979; Greimas and Courtés 1976, 1982;
Hutcheon 1985; Kerbrat-Orecchioni 1980;
Lejeune 1975, 1982.

enunciator. An ADDRESSER. Should I tell
someone a story, I am its enunciator, and
should he or she tell me a story in return,
he or she is its enunciator. ¶Greimas and
Courtés 1976, 1982.

epic preterite. The preterite characteristic of
epic or fictional narrative. According to
Käte Hamburger, this so-called epic preterite (EPISCHE PRAETERITUM) is a distinctive
feature of fiction as opposed to nonfiction
(or of FIKTIONALE ERZÄHLEN as opposed to
AUSSAGE): rather than signifying real time,
rather than labelling the situations and
events reported as past, it designates them
as fictive (the past exists only for a real
person; events in fiction are "time-less"
and "occur" in the characters' fictive and
"time-less" present). For Hamburger, this
special status of the epic preterite is evi-
denced by combinations between it and
DEICTIC (temporal) adverbials that would be
unacceptable in statements about reality:
consider, for example, "He saw her, and
now he felt bad," in which an adverbial
form designating a present is combined

with a preterite. ¶Some students of narrative (Bronzwaer, Chatman) have argued that Hamburger's claim is excessive and, more specifically, that the co-occurrence of preterite tense forms and deictic (temporal) adverbials does not define fictionality. Others, however, have argued—not unlike Hamburger—that, in fiction, the preterite constitutes a present with esthetic distance and expresses above all the fictional status of the world represented (Ingarden, Sartre, Barthes). ¶Banfield 1982; Barthes 1968; Bronzwaer 1970; Chatman 1978; Hamburger 1973; Ingarden 1973; Pascal 1962; Ricoeur 1985; Sartre 1965; Weinrich 1964.

epilogue. A final section in some narratives, coming after the DENOUEMENT and not to be confused with it. The epilogue helps to realize fully the design of the work. ¶Martin 1986. See also PROLOGUE.

epische Praeteritum. See EPIC PRETERITE. ¶Hamburger 1973.

episode. A series of related events standing apart from surrounding (series of) events because of one or more distinctive features and having a unity. ¶Beaugrande 1980; Brooks and Warren 1959. See also GOAL, STORY GRAMMAR.

episodic plot. A loosely woven PLOT; a plot in which no strong causal continuity exists between one EVENT or EPISODE and the next; a plot the events or episodes of which have no necessary or probable relation to each other. ¶Aristotle 1968; Brooks and Warren 1959.

Er-Form. THIRD-PERSON NARRATIVE form (he-form). ¶Doležel 1973; Füger 1972. See also ICH-FORM, DU-FORM.

erlebendes Ich. The experiencing "I" in HOMODIEGETIC NARRATIVE, the CHARACTER-I (as opposed to ERZÄHLENDES ICH, the narrating "I," the NARRATOR-I). In "I felt bad," the subject pronoun refers both to an *erlebendes Ich* (the one who felt) and to an *erzählendes Ich* (the one who tells about the feeling); and in *Nausea,* Roquentin is an *erlebendes Ich* insofar as he longs to see Anny again and an *erzählendes Ich* insofar as he recounts the longing in his diary. ¶Lämmert 1955; Spitzer 1928.

erlebte rede. FREE INDIRECT DISCOURSE. ¶The term, first used by Etienne Lorck, literally means "experienced speech." ¶Lorck 1921; Pascal 1977.

erzählendes Ich. In HOMODIEGETIC NARRATIVE the "I" who narrates, the NARRATOR-I (as opposed to ERLEBENDES ICH, the "I" who experiences, the CHARACTER-I). In "I saw her come out of the room," the subject pronoun refers both to an *erzählendes Ich* (the one who tells about the seeing) and to an *erlebendes Ich* (the one who saw); and in *Great Expectations,* Pip is an *erzählendes Ich* insofar as he recounts his adventures and an *erlebendes Ich* insofar as he lives them. ¶Lämmert 1955; Spitzer 1928.

erzählte Welt. According to Weinrich, one of two distinct and complementary categories of textual worlds, comprising the various kinds of verbal narrative and in English signaled by the use of such forms as the preterite, the imperfect, and the pluperfect. With the *erzählte Welt* (narrated world) category, as opposed to the BESPROCHENE WELT (commented world) category, the ADDRESSER and ADDRESSEE do not (seem to) consider themselves directly linked to and concerned by what is described. ¶Weinrich's distinction between *erzählte Welt* and *besprochene Welt* is analogous to Benveniste's distinction between HISTOIRE and DISCOURS and is related to Hamburger's distinction between FIKTIONALE ERZÄHLEN and AUSSAGE. ¶Ricoeur 1985; Weinrich 1964. See also TENSE.

Erzählte Zeit. The STORY TIME; the time span covered by the situations and events represented (as opposed to ERZÄHLZEIT). ¶Müller 1968. See also DURATION, SPEED.

Erzählzeit. The DISCOURSE TIME; the time taken by the representation of situations and events (as opposed to ERZÄHLTE ZEIT). ¶Müller 1968. See also DURATION, SPEED.

ethos. See CHARACTER. ¶Aristotle 1968.

etic approach. An external and taxonomic (as opposed to an emic or internal and functional) approach to the study of (human) situations and productions. Rather than defining and describing the constituents of a system from the point of view of one familiar with it, the etic approach uses criteria not intrinsic to the system to do it. ¶Kenneth Pike coined the term *etic* by analogy with the term *phonetic*. ¶Dundes 1962, 1964; Pike 1967. See also EMIC APPROACH.

evaluation. In Labov's terminology, the set of features in a NARRATIVE that indicate or suggest its POINT; the aspects of a narrative that show why the situations and events narrated are worth narrating. In "I thought to myself that it was extremely bizarre," "The car stopped. The car stopped and a woman got out," "He didn't say anything: he just stood there," and "The point of my story is that people are basically

nice," for example, the narrator's reflection (emphasizing the unusual quality of the happenings), the repetition (suggesting the importance of the event), the negative (underlining what did obtain as opposed to what could have), and the explicit statement of the point all function as evaluative devices and are part of the evaluation. ¶Culler 1981; Labov 1972; Pratt 1977. See also COMMENTARY, REPORTABILITY.

event. A change of STATE manifested in DISCOURSE by a PROCESS STATEMENT in the mode of *Do* or *Happen*. An event can be an ACTION or ACT (when the change is brought about by an agent: "Mary opened the window") or a HAPPENING (when the change is not brought about by an agent: "the rain started to fall"). ¶Along with EXISTENTS, events are the fundamental constituents of the STORY. ¶Chatman 1978; van Dijk 1974–75.

existent. An ACTOR or an item of SETTING: the subject and object of "Susan looked at the table" designate existents. ¶Along with EVENTS, existents are the fundamental constituents of the STORY. ¶Chatman 1978.

exposition. The presentation of the circumstances obtaining before the BEGINNING of the action. In many narratives, there is a delayed exposition: the expository information is provided after the beginning of the action has been set forth. ¶Brooks and Warren 1959; Freytag 1894; Sternberg 1974, 1978; Tomashevsky 1965. See also FREYTAG'S PYRAMID.

expression. Following Hjelmslev, one of the two planes of any semiotic system: the "way" something is signified as opposed to the "what" that is signified. Like the CON-

TENT plane, the expression plane has a FORM and a SUBSTANCE. ¶When used in connection with narrative, expression can be said to be equivalent to DISCOURSE (as opposed to STORY). ¶Chatman 1978; Hjelmslev 1954, 1961; Prince 1973.

expressive function. See EMOTIVE FUNCTION. ¶K. Bühler 1934; Jakobson 1960.

extension. The duration of each constituent unit in an ITERATIVE NARRATIVE; the span of time covered by an event (or set of events) that is said to recur: "I studied every day from noon to midnight" is an iterative narrative with an extension of twelve hours. ¶Genette 1980.

extent. The duration or AMPLITUDE of an ANACHRONY; the STORY TIME covered by it. ¶Genette 1980.

external action. What characters say and do as opposed to what they think or feel (INTERNAL ACTION). ¶Brooks and Warren 1959.

external focalization. 1. A type of FOCALIZATION or POINT OF VIEW whereby the information conveyed is mostly limited to what the characters do and say and there is never any direct indication of what they think or feel. External focalization is characteristic of the so-called OBJECTIVE or BEHAVIORIST NARRATIVE ("Hills Like White Elephants"), and one of its consequences is that the NARRATOR tells less than one or several characters know. ¶Several narratologists have argued that external focalization is defined in terms of a criterion different from the one characterizing ZERO FOCALIZATION or INTERNAL FOCALIZATION (nature of what is perceived, of the information conveyed, as opposed to position of the perceiver). In a discussion of this problem, Genette, who coined the term, specifies that with external focalization, the FOCALIZER is situated in the DIEGESIS (*diégèse*) but outside any of the characters, thereby excluding the possibility of information on any thoughts or feelings. 2. NONFOCALIZATION or zero focalization in Rimmon-Kenan's terminology. ¶Bal 1977, 1983, 1985; Genette 1980, 1983; Lintvelt 1981; Rimmon-Kenan 1983. See also DRAMATIC MODE, VISION.

external plot. A PLOT based on outer events and experiences, as in adventure stories. ¶H. James 1972. See also INTERNAL PLOT.

external point of view. See EXTERNAL FOCALIZATION. ¶Prince 1982; Uspenskij 1973.

extradiegetic. External to (not part of) any DIEGESIS (*diégèse*). The NARRATOR of *Eugénie Grandet* is an extradiegetic narrator. More generally, the narrator of a PRIMARY NARRATIVE is always extradiegetic. ¶An extradiegetic narrator is not equivalent to a HETERODIEGETIC one. Thus, in *Arabian Nights,* Scheherazade functions as a heterodiegetic narrator (since she does not tell her own story) and as an INTRADIEGETIC rather than extradiegetic one (since she is a character in a framing narrative that she does not tell). Conversely, in *Gil Blas,* the narrator is a HOMODIEGETIC and extradiegetic one (he tells his own story, but as narrator, he is not part of any diegesis). ¶Genette 1980, 1983; Lanser 1981; Rimmon 1976. See also DIEGETIC LEVEL.

fabula. The set of narrated situations and events in their chronological sequence; the basic STORY material (as opposed to PLOT or SJUŽET), in Russian Formalist terminology. ¶Chatman 1978; Ejxenbaum 1971b; Erlich 1965.

falling action. Along with the RISING ACTION and the CLIMAX, one of the basic constituents of a (dramatic or closely knit) PLOT structure. The falling action follows the climax and extends to the DENOUEMENT. ¶Freytag 1894. See also FREYTAG'S PYRAMID.

false hero. One of the seven fundamental ROLES that a character may assume (in a fairy tale), according to Propp. The false hero (analogous to Greimas's OPPONENT and Souriau's MARS) pretends to have accomplished what, in fact, the HERO accomplished. ¶Propp 1968. See also ACTANT, DRAMATIS PERSONA, SPHERE OF ACTION.

ficelle. A term used by Henry James to designate a CHARACTER whose main function is to throw light on the meaning or significance of the situations and events narrated. Henrietta Stackpole in *The Portrait of a Lady* and Maria Gostrey in *The Ambassadors* are *ficelles*. ¶The term means "string" in French, as well as "trick" or "ruse" (cf. the strings with which a puppeteer controls his or her puppets). ¶Booth 1983; H. James 1972; Souvage 1965.

fiction. STORY, in Ricardou's terminology, as opposed to NARRATION or DISCOURSE. ¶Ricardou 1967.

figural narrative situation. One of Stanzel's three basic types of NARRATIVE SITUATION, along with the AUTHORIAL NARRATIVE SITUATION (AUKTORIALE ERZÄHLSITUATION) and the FIRST-PERSON NARRATIVE SITUATION (ICH ERZÄHLSITUATION). The figural (or PERSONAL) NARRATIVE SITUATION (PERSONALE ERZÄHLSITUATION) is characterized by INTERNAL FOCALIZATION (and a NARRATOR who is not a participant in the situations and events recounted: *The Ambassadors*). ¶Stanzel 1964, 1971, 1984.

figure. The entity or collection of entities focused on or foregrounded. A figure comes to the fore against a GROUND or BACKGROUND. ¶Beaugrande 1980; Chatman 1978. See also FOREGROUND.

fiktionale Erzählen. One of two linguistic subsystems, according to Hamburger, who opposes it to what she calls AUSSAGE (statement). *Fiktionale Erzählen* (fictional recounting) consists of THIRD-PERSON NARRATIVE fiction. Whereas the statements constituting *Aussage* are relatable to a real (or feigned) I-Origo, a real (or feigned) originary "I" and his or her subjectivity, in *fiktionale Erzählen,* fictive characters introduced as third persons are the subjects of the utterances, thoughts, feelings, and actions presented. Furthermore, the basic tense used in *fiktionale Erzählen*—the preterite—designates as fictive the situations and events reported rather than labelling them as past (the past exists only for an I-Origo; situations and events in fiction are "time-less"). Finally, *fiktionale Erzählen* has the unique ability to portray the subjectivity of third persons *qua* third persons: it is the only place where such a subjectivity can be presented, the only place where a third person's mind can be inspected from the inside. ¶Hamburger's distinction between *fiktionale Erzählen* and *Aussage* is analogous though by no means equivalent to Benveniste's distinction between HISTOIRE and DISCOURS and Weinrich's distinction between ERZÄHLTE WELT and BESPROCHENE WELT. ¶Banfield 1982; Hamburger 1973. See also EPIC PRETERITE.

first-person narrative. A narrative the NARRATOR of which is a character in the situations and events recounted (and, in the latter capacity, is designated by an "I"). Sartre's *The Words* is a first-person narrative, and so are Joinville's *Memoirs,* Augustine's *Confessions,* and Robinson Crusoe's account of his adventures. ¶Głowiński 1977; Prince 1982; Romberg 1982; Rousset 1973; Tamir 1976. See also HOMODIEGETIC NARRATIVE, PERSON.

first-person narrative situation. One of Stanzel's three basic types of NARRATIVE SITUATION, along with the AUTHORIAL NARRATIVE SITUATION (AUKTORIALE ERZÄHLSITUATION) and the FIGURAL NARRATIVE SITUATION (PERSONALE ERZÄHLSITUATION). The first-person narrative situation (ICH ERZÄHLSITUATION) is characterized by a narrator who is a participant in the situations and events recounted (*Great Expectations, Moll Flanders, Lord Jim*). ¶Stanzel 1964, 1971, 1984. See also HOMODIEGETIC NARRATIVE.

fixed internal focalization. A type of INTERNAL FOCALIZATION such that one and only one character is the FOCALIZER; a rendering of situations and events in terms of one and only one POINT OF VIEW (*The Ambassadors*). ¶Genette 1980. See also FOCALIZATION.

fixed internal point of view. See FIXED INTERNAL FOCALIZATION. ¶Prince 1982.

flashback. An ANALEPSIS; a RETROSPECTION; a CUTBACK; a SWITCHBACK. The term is often used in connection with cinematic narrative. (*Citizen Kane, The Locket, Wild Strawberries*). ¶Chatman 1978; Prince 1982; Souvage 1965. See also ANACHRONY, ORDER.

flashforward. A PROLEPSIS; an ANTICIPATION. The term is often used in connection with cinematic narrative (*The Anderson Tapes; Petulia; They Shoot Horses, Don't They?*). ¶Chatman 1978; Prince 1982. See also ADVANCE NOTICE, ANACHRONY, ORDER.

flat character. A CHARACTER endowed with one or very few TRAITS and highly predictable in behavior. Mrs. Micawber in *David Copperfield* is a flat character. ¶Forster 1927. See also ROUND CHARACTER.

focal character. The character in terms of whose POINT OF VIEW the narrated situations and events are presented; the character as FOCALIZER; the VIEWPOINT CHARACTER. In *The Ambassadors,* Strether is the focal character.

focalization. The PERSPECTIVE in terms of which the narrated situations and events are presented; the perceptual or conceptual position in terms of which they are rendered (Genette). When such a position varies and is sometimes unlocatable (when no systematic conceptual or perceptual constraint governs what may be presented), the narrative is said to have ZERO FOCALIZATION or to be nonfocalized: zero focalization is characteristic of "traditional" or "classical" narrative (*Vanity Fair, Adam Bede*) and associated with so-called OMNISCIENT NARRATORS. When such a position is locatable (in one character or another) and entails conceptual or perceptual restrictions (with what is presented being governed by one character's or another's perspective), the narrative is said to have INTERNAL FOCALIZATION (*The Ambassadors, The Age of Reason, The Ring and the Book*). Internal focalization can be fixed (when one and only one perspective is adopted: *The Ambassadors, What Maisie Knew*), variable (when different perspectives are adopted in turn to present different situations and events: *The Age of Reason, The Golden Bowl*), or multiple (when the same situations and events are presented more than once, each time in terms of a different perspective: *The Ring and the Book, The Moonstone, Rashomon*). Should what is presented be limited to the characters' external behavior (words and actions but not thoughts or feelings), their appearance, and the setting against which they come to the fore, EXTERNAL FOCALIZATION is said to obtain ("The Killers"). Several narratologists have argued that external focalization is characterized not so much by the perspective adopted as by the information provided. Indeed, if a given character's perspective is adopted (internal focalization), it may well happen that only words and actions but not thoughts or feelings are presented (external focalization).

In a discussion of this problem, Genette specifies that in the case of external focalization, the FOCALIZER is situated in the DIEGESIS (*diégèse*) but outside any of the characters. ¶Focalization—"who sees" or, more generally, "who perceives (and conceives)"—should be distinguished from VOICE ("who speaks," "who tells," "who narrates"). ¶Bal 1977, 1981a, 1983, 1985; Genette 1980, 1983; Rimmon-Kenan 1983; Vitoux 1982. See also ASPECT, DOUBLE FOCALIZATION, FIXED INTERNAL FOCALIZATION, FOCALIZED, MULTIPLE INTERNAL FOCALIZATION, NONFOCALIZATION, POINT OF VIEW, VARIABLE INTERNAL FOCALIZATION, VISION.

focalized. The object of FOCALIZATION; the existent or event presented in terms of the FOCALIZER's perspective. In "Jane saw Peter leaning against the chair. He looked strange to her," Peter is the focalized. ¶Bal 1977, 1983, 1985; Martin 1986; Vitoux 1982.

focalizer. The subject of FOCALIZATION; the holder of POINT OF VIEW; the focal point governing the focalization. In "Jane saw Peter leaning against the chair. He looked strange to her," Jane is the focalizer. ¶Bal 1977, 1983, 1985; Lanser 1981; Martin 1986; Vitoux 1982. See also CENTRAL CONSCIOUSNESS, FOCAL CHARACTER, FOCALIZED.

focus of narration. The VOICE and POINT OF VIEW governing the situations and events presented. Brooks and Warren distinguish four NARRATIVE SITUATIONS, four narrational types corresponding to four basic focuses of narration: (1) first-person (a character tells his or her own story); (2) first-person observer (a character tells a story which s/he has observed); (3) author-observer (a

HETERODIEGETIC NARRATOR limits what s/he tells to the characters' words and actions); (4) omniscient author (a heterodiegetic narrator tells what happens, and s/he has the freedom to enter the characters' minds and to comment on the action). Types 1 and 2 correspond to HOMODIEGETIC NARRATIVES with INTERNAL FOCALIZATION, type 3 to HETERODIEGETIC NARRATIVES with EXTERNAL FOCALIZATION (BEHAVIORIST NARRATIVE, DRAMATIC MODE), and type 4 to HETERODIEGETIC NARRATIVES with ZERO FOCALIZATION (OMNISCIENT NARRATOR). ¶Brooks and Warren 1959.

foreground. That which is focused on, underlined, emphasized; that which comes to the fore against a BACKGROUND. ¶Weinrich 1964. See also FIGURE, GROUND.

foreshadowing. The technique or device whereby some situation or event is hinted at in advance. For example, should a character manifest extreme sensitivity to color as a child and then become a famous painter, the first event is said to foreshadow the second. ¶Brooks and Warren 1959; Chatman 1978; Souvage 1965. See also ADVANCE MENTION, SUSPENSE.

foreshortening. See SUMMARY. ¶Brooks and Warren 1959; H. James 1972.

form. Following Hjelmslev, and as opposed to SUBSTANCE, the relational system determining the units of the two planes of a semiotic system (the EXPRESSION plane and the CONTENT plane). ¶In the case of narrative, the form of the content can be said to be equivalent to the STORY components (existents and events) and their connections; and the form of the expression to the constituents (NARRATIVE

STATEMENTS) that state the story and, more specifically, determine the ORDER of presentation, the narrative SPEED, the kind of COMMENTARY, and so on. ¶Chatman 1978; Ducrot and Todorov 1979; Hjelmslev 1954, 1961.

frame. A set of related mental data representing various aspects of reality and enabling human perception and comprehension of these aspects (Minsky). A "restaurant" frame, for example, is a network of data pertaining to the parts, function, etc., that restaurants typically have. More generally, NARRATIVE can be considered a frame allowing for certain kinds of organization and understandings of reality. ¶Frames are often taken to be equivalent to SCHEMATA, PLANS, and SCRIPTS, but certain suggestive distinctions have been proposed: a serially ordered, temporally bound frame is a schema; a goal-directed schema is a plan; and a stereotypical plan is a script. ¶Beaugrande 1980; Goffman 1974; Minsky 1975; Schank and Abelson 1977; Winograd 1975.

frame narrative. A narrative in which another narrative is embedded; a narrative functioning as a frame for another narrative by providing a setting for it. In *Manon Lescaut,* M. de Renoncourt's narrative is a frame narrative. ¶See also EMBEDDED NARRATIVE, EMBEDDING, METADIEGETIC NARRATIVE.

free clause. A clause the DISPLACEMENT SET of which is equal to the entire narrative; a clause unaffected by TEMPORAL JUNCTURE and therefore displaceable without any resulting change in the semantic interpretation. In "The birds kepts on singing. John was happy; then he thought about Mary," "The birds kept on singing" is a free clause. ¶Labov 1972; Labov and Waletzky 1967. See also COORDINATE CLAUSES, NARRATIVE CLAUSE, RESTRICTED CLAUSE.

free direct discourse. A TYPE OF DISCOURSE whereby a character's utterances or thoughts are (presumably) given as the character formulates them, without any narratorial mediation (TAGS, quotation marks, dashes, etc.). In "It was unbearably hot, and she just stood there. I can't stand any of these people! She decided to leave," "I can't stand any of these people" is an instance of free direct discourse. ¶Free direct discourse sometimes is also made to cover those cases in which a character's perceptions are presented directly as they occur in his or her consciousness. ¶Chatman 1978; Genette 1980, 1983; Lanser 1981; Todorov 1981. See also DIRECT DISCOURSE, IMMEDIATE DISCOURSE, INTERIOR MONOLOGUE, STREAM OF CONSCIOUSNESS.

free direct speech. FREE DIRECT DISCOURSE, especially free direct discourse whereby a character's utterances (as opposed to thoughts) are presented. ¶Chatman 1978. See also FREE DIRECT THOUGHT.

free direct style. See FREE DIRECT DISCOURSE.

free direct thought. FREE DIRECT DISCOURSE whereby a character's thoughts (as opposed to utterances) are presented. It is often called INTERIOR MONOLOGUE when in extended form. ¶Chatman 1978; Scholes and Kellogg 1966. See also FREE DIRECT SPEECH.

free indirect discourse. A TYPE OF DISCOURSE representing a character's utterances or thoughts. Free indirect discourse (NARRATED MONOLOGUE, REPRESENTED SPEECH AND THOUGHT, STYLE INDIRECT LIBRE, ERLEBTE REDE, SUBSTITUTIONARY NARRATION) has the grammatical traits of "normal" INDIRECT DISCOURSE, but it does not involve a TAG CLAUSE ("he said that," "she thought that") introducing and qualifying the represented utterances and thoughts. Furthermore, it manifests at least some of the features of the character's ENUNCIATION (some of the features normally associated with the discourse of a character presented directly, with a first person's as opposed to a third person's discourse: compare "He became indignant. A man like him was a suspect now!" or "She smiled. Mary, bless her soul, would be coming to relieve her tomorrow" with "He became indignant: 'A man like me is a suspect now!' " or "She smiled: 'Mary, bless her soul, will be coming to relieve me tomorrow' "). Free indirect discourse—which is not linguistically derivable from DIRECT DISCOURSE or ("normal") TAGGED INDIRECT DISCOURSE—is usually taken to contain mixed within it markers of two discourse events (a narrator's and a character's), two styles, two languages, two voices, two semantic and axiological systems. However, some theorists (e.g., Banfield) have argued—*contra* this DUAL VOICE HYPOTHESIS—that it should be taken to be a speakerless (narratorless) representation of one subjectivity or self. ¶There are a number of grammatical features or indices that might characterize a particular passage as free indirect discourse (back-shift of tenses, conversion of personal and possessive pronouns, DEICTICS referring to the character's spatiotemporal frame, etc.). These grammatical features, however, do not appear in every instance of free indirect discourse (and do not by themselves guarantee its being unequivocally distinguished from NARRATIZED DISCOURSE). In other words, free indirect discourse is not definable in strictly grammatical terms. It is also (and perhaps more frequently) a function of what might be called contextual features: (1)formal features such as general markers of colloquialism (ejaculations, lexical fillers, evaluative expressions, emotive elements, subjective indicators normally absent from narratorial discourse); more specific markers of a group or class to which a character belongs; even more specific markers of a character's personal idiom (distinctive words, registers, "intonations"); or markers of social-role relationships (for example, appellations which would be used only by particular characters with respect to other characters); and (2) semantic features (assessments, interpretations, judgments, "intended meanings" more plausibly attributable to a character than to the narrator). So dependent is free indirect discourse on context that it appears more readily in the vicinity of verbs of speech or thought, or next to instances of direct or indirect discourse, or in the neighborhood of a foregrounded character. ¶Though free indirect discourse may have a special affinity with the third person, it can and does occur in the first and second persons ("My dream was out; my wild fancy was surpassed by sober reality; Miss Havisham was going to make my fortune on a grand scale"). Though it may favor past tenses, it can and does make room for other tenses ("She shrugs her shoulders and goes out. She's not gonna fall for this two-bit punk"). Though it often co-occurs with INTERNAL FOCALIZATION, it clearly does not appear in every passage presented in terms of a given character's perspective (consider, for example, "He saw John leaning against the wall" or "She thought about her past and felt deeply moved"). Finally, though it occurs perhaps more frequently in written language, it can and does occur in spoken language. ¶The category of free indirect discourse is sometimes extended to include discourse representing a character's nonverbalized perceptions as they occur in his or her consciousness (REPRESENTED PERCEPTION). Compare "Mary just stood there. The man was crawling toward her" and "Mary just stood there and saw the man crawling toward her." ¶Bakhtin 1981; Bal 1977, 1985; Bally 1912; Banfield 1982; W. Bühler 1937; Chatman 1978; Cohn 1978; Dillon and Kirchhoff 1976; Genette 1980, 1983; Jespersen 1924; Lips 1926; Lorck 1921; McHale 1978, 1983; Pascal 1977; Strauch 1974; Todorov 1981; Vološinov 1973.

free indirect speech. FREE INDIRECT DISCOURSE, especially free indirect discourse whereby a character's utterances (as opposed to thoughts) are represented. ¶Chatman 1978. See also FREE INDIRECT THOUGHT.

free indirect style. See FREE INDIRECT DISCOURSE.

free indirect thought. FREE INDIRECT DISCOURSE whereby a character's thoughts (as opposed to utterances) are represented. ¶Chatman 1978. See also FREE INDIRECT SPEECH.

free motif. A CATALYSIS; a SATELLITE; a minor event in a PLOT. For Tomashevsky and the Russian Formalists, free motifs (as opposed to BOUND MOTIFS) are not logically essential to the narrative action, and their elimination does not alter its causal-chronological coherence. ¶Ducrot and Todorov 1979; Tomashevsky 1965. See also MOTIF.

frequency. The relationship between the number of times an event happens and the number of times it is recounted. For example, I can recount once what happened once or *n* times what happened *n* times (SINGULATIVE NARRATIVE); I can recount *n* times what happened once (REPEATING NARRATIVE); and I can recount once what happened *n* times (ITERATIVE NARRATIVE). ¶Genette 1980, 1983; Rimmon-Kenan 1983.

Freytag's pyramid. Gustav Freytag's diagrammatic representation of the structure of a tragedy:

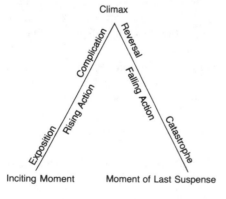

Freytag's pyramid has often been used to characterize (various aspects of) PLOT in narrative. ¶Freytag 1894.

function. 1. An ACT defined in terms of its significance for the course of the ACTION in which it appears; an act considered in terms of the role it plays at the action level; a MOTIFEME. Propp, who developed the notion in his study of the (Russian) folktale, showed that the same act can have different roles (be subsumed by different functions) in different tales ("John killed Peter," for instance, might constitute a villainy in one tale and the hero's victory in another); conversely, different acts can have the same role (be subsumed by the same function) in different tales ("John killed Peter" and "The dragon kidnapped the princess," for example, might both constitute a villainy). For Propp, functions constitute the fundamental components of the underlying structure of any (Russian) fairy tale; furthermore, no function excludes any other and, however many of them appear in a single tale, they always appear in the same order (given the set *a, b, c, d, e, . . . , n,* should *b, c,* and *e* appear in a particular tale, they will appear in that order); finally, their number is limited to thirty-one, which Propp describes as follows:

I. One of the members of a family absents himself from home (*absentation*).

II. An interdiction is addressed to the hero (*interdiction*).

III. The interdiction is violated (*violation*).

IV. The villain makes an attempt at reconnaissance (*reconnaissance*).

V. The villain receives information about his victim (*delivery*).

VI. The villain attempts to deceive his victim in order to take possession of him or his belongings (*trickery*).

VII. The victim submits to deception and thereby unwittingly helps his enemy (*complicity*).

VIII. The villain causes harm or injury to a member of a family (*villainy*).

VIIIa. One member of a family either lacks something or desires to have something (*lack*).

IX. Misfortune or lack is made known; the hero is approached with a request or command; he is allowed to go or he is dispatched (*mediation, the connective incident*).

X. The seeker agrees to or decides upon counteraction (*beginning counteraction*).

XI. The hero leaves home (*departure*).

XII. The hero is tested, interrogated, attacked, etc., which prepares the way for his receiving either a magical agent or helper (*the first function of the donor*).

XIII. The hero reacts to the actions of the future donor (*the hero's reaction*).

XIV. The hero acquires the use of a magical agent (*provision or receipt of a magical agent*).

XV. The hero is transferred, delivered, or led to the whereabouts of an object of search (*spatial transference between two kingdoms, guidance*).

XVI. The hero and the villain join in direct combat (*struggle*).

XVII. The hero is branded (*branding, marking*).

XVIII. The villain is defeated (*victory*).

XIX. The initial misfortune or lack is liquidated (*liquidation of misfortune or lack*).

XX. The hero returns (*return*).

XXI. The hero is pursued (*pursuit, chase*).

XXII. Rescue of the hero from pursuit (*rescue*).

XXIII. The hero, unrecognized, arrives home or in another country (*unrecognized arrival*).

XXIV. The hero, unrecognized, arrives home or in another country (*unrecognized arrival*).

XXIV. A false hero presents unfounded claims (*unfounded claims*).

XXV. A difficult task is proposed to the hero (*difficult task*).

XXVI. The task is resolved (*solution*).

XXVII. The hero is recognized (*recognition*).

XXVIII. The false hero or villain is exposed (*exposure*).

XXIX. The hero is given a new appearance (*transfiguration*).

XXX. The villain is punished (*punishment*).

XXXI. The hero is married and ascends the throne (*wedding*).

Propp's functional account is often considered to mark the birth of modern NARRATOLOGY and the STRUCTURAL ANALYSIS OF NARRATIVE and it has constituted a starting point for many influential models of narrative structure. Thus, Greimas's NARRATIVE SCHEMA ultimately results from a reanalysis of Proppian functions, and Bremond's characterization of narrative as combinations of SEQUENCES or TRIADS is articulated along functional lines.   **2.** A narrative unit or MOTIF metonymically related to other units in the same sequence or action (linked to them in terms of consecution or consequence). Barthes contrasted the function and the INDEX, which is metaphorically rather than metonymically related to other units (linked to them in terms other than chronological or causal: for instance, thematic ones), and he distinguished two kinds of function: CARDINAL FUNCTIONS and CATALYSES. ¶The same unit can constitute a function and an index.   **3.** In Greimas's early model of narrative, a dynamic PREDICATE (as opposed to the QUALIFICATION or static predicate).   **4.** A fundamental ROLE or ACTANT, in Souriau's terminology. The six functions are the LION, the SUN, the EARTH, MARS, the BALANCE, and the MOON. ¶Barthes 1975; Bremond 1973, 1980, 1982; Culler 1975; Greimas 1970, 1983a, 1983b; Greimas and Courtés 1982; Hénault 1983; Propp 1968; Scholes 1974; Souriau 1950. See also METONYMY, MOVE.

functions of communication. The directions orienting any act of (verbal) communication and determining the roles it fulfills. Each function corresponds to one of the CONSTITUTIVE FACTORS OF COMMUNICATION, and any communicative act fulfills one or more functions. ¶Bühler had isolated three functions of language:

REPRESENTATIVE, APPELLATIVE, and EXPRESSIVE. Jakobson, in what has proven to be the most influential model of (verbal) communication in NARRATOLOGY, proposed a schema involving six functions: (1) the EMOTIVE FUNCTION, related to an emphasis on the ADDRESSER; (2) the CONATIVE FUNCTION, related to an emphasis on the ADDRESSEE; (3) the REFERENTIAL FUNCTION, related to an emphasis on the CONTEXT or REFERENT; (4) the PHATIC FUNCTION, related to an emphasis on the CONTACT; (5) the POETIC FUNCTION, related to an emphasis on the MESSAGE for its own sake; and (6) the METALINGUAL FUNCTION, related to an emphasis on the CODE:

Referential
Poetic
Emotive_____Conative
Phatic
Metalingual

¶K. Bühler 1934; Jakobson 1960.

generative trajectory. The general economy of the component parts of a semiotic theory, according to Greimassian terminology. In a generative trajectory (*parcours génératif*), the component parts are articulated along a path that goes from the simple to the complex and the abstract to the concrete. For instance, Greimas's model of narrative—whereby two basic components (syntactic and semantic) are generated (assigned a description) along two narrative levels (deep and surface) and one discursive level—can be represented by the diagram below (to be read from top to bottom). ¶Greimas and Courtés 1982; Hénault 1983.

glorifying test. One of the three TESTS characterizing the movement of the SUBJECT in the canonical NARRATIVE SCHEMA. Presupposing the DECISIVE TEST which in turn presupposes the QUALIFYING TEST, the glorifying test results in the recognition of the Subject's accomplishment and (usually) takes place when the decisive test has occurred in secret. ¶Greimas 1983a, 1983b; Greimas and Courtés 1982; Hénault 1983. See also SANCTION.

gnarus. A Latin word meaning "knowing," "expert," "acquainted with," and deriving from the Indo-European root gnâ ("to know"). Such words as NARRATOR, *narrate,* NARRATIVE, etc., are related to it: etymologically speaking, the narrator is the one who knows. ¶Mitchell 1981.

gnomic code. See REFERENTIAL CODE. ¶Barthes 1974.

goal. A desired final state for a character.

STORY GRAMMARS take a story to consist of a series of EPISODES which bring a character closer to or farther from the goal through the reaching or not reaching of a SUBGOAL. ¶Beaugrande 1980; Black and Bower 1980; Rumelhart 1975; Thorndyke 1977.

goal-state. See GOAL.

ground. The entity or collection of entities against which another entity or collection of entities (a FIGURE) emerges and comes to the fore. ¶Beaugrande 1980; Chatman 1978. See also BACKGROUND, FOREGROUND

happening. Along with the ACT or ACTION, one of two possible kinds of narrated EVENTS; a change of state not brought about by an AGENT and manifested in discourse by a PROCESS STATEMENT in the mode of *Happen.* "It started to rain" and "Mary was hit by a falling rock" represent happenings. ¶Chatman 1978. See also

GENERATIVE TRAJECTORY			
		Syntactic Component	Semantic Component
Semio-Narrative Structures	Deep Level	Fundamental Syntax	Fundamental Semantics
	Surface Level	Narrative Surface Syntax	Narrative Semantics
Discursive Structures		Discursive Syntax Discursivization | Temporalization Actorialization Spatialization	Discursive Semantics Thematization Figurativization

NARRATIVE STATEMENT.

helper. 1. One of the seven fundamental ROLES that a character may assume (in a fairy tale), according to Propp; one of six ACTANTS in Greimas's early versions of the ACTANTIAL MODEL. The Helper (analogous to Souriau's MOON) helps the HERO or SUBJECT. **2.** In Greimas's more recent model of narrative, a positive AUXILIANT that is represented, at the surface structure level, by an ACTOR different form the one representing the Subject. ¶Greimas 1970, 1983b; Greimas and Courtés 1982; Hénault 1983; Propp 1968. See also DRAMATIS PERSONA, SPHERE OF ACTION.

hermeneuteme. A unit of the HERMENEUTIC CODE; an element in terms of which the path from an enigma to its solution is articulated. Barthes isolated the following hermeneutemes: thematization (underlining what will be the object of the enigma); proposal (signaling the existence of an enigma); formulation (of the enigma); promise or request for an answer; snare (false lead, deliberate evasion of truth); equivocation (mixture of truth and snare); jamming (admitting the insolubility of the enigma); suspended answer; disclosure or decipherment. ¶Barthes 1974. See also SUSPENSE.

hermeneutic code. The CODE or "voice" according to which a narrative or part thereof can be structured as a path leading from a question or enigma to its (possible) answer or solution. ¶A passage can signify in terms of the hermeneutic code if it suggests or asserts that there is a question to be asked or an enigma to be solved; if it formulates that question or enigma; if it announces or alludes to a (possible) answer or solution; or if it constitutes that answer or solution, represents a contribution to it, or acts as an obstacle to it. ¶Barthes 1974, 1981a; Culler 1975; Prince 1982. See also HERMENEUTEME.

hero. 1. The PROTAGONIST or central character in a narrative. The hero (or heroine) usually represents positive values. **2.** One of the seven fundamental ROLES that a character may assume (in a fairy tale), according to Propp. The hero (analogous to Greimas's SUBJECT and Souriau's LION) suffers from the action of the VILLAIN or from some kind of lack and/or liquidates his or another character's misfortune or lack. ¶Hamon 1972, 1983; Propp 1968. See also ACTANT, ANTIHERO, DRAMATIS PERSONA, SPHERE OF ACTION.

heterodiegetic narrative. A narrative the NARRATOR of which is not a character in the situations and events recounted; a narrative with a HETERODIEGETIC NARRATOR. The *Iliad, Tom Jones, A Tale of Two Cities,* and *The Decline and Fall of the Roman Empire* are heterodiegetic (as opposed to HOMODIEGETIC) NARRATIVES. ¶Genette 1980, 1983. See also DIEGETIC, EXTRADIEGETIC, INTRADIEGETIC, PERSON, THIRD-PERSON NARRATIVE.

heterodiegetic narrator. A NARRATOR who is not part of the DIEGESIS (*diégèse*) s/he presents; a narrator who is not a character in the situations and events s/he recounts. The narrators in *Eugénie Grandet,* the *Iliad,* and Carlyle's *French Revolution* are heterodiegetic. ¶Genette 1980, 1983; Lanser 1981. See also EXTRADIEGETIC, HETERODIEGETIC NARRATIVE, HOMODIEGETIC NARRATOR.

histoire. See STORY. ¶Benveniste 1971.

homodiegetic narrative. A narrative the NARRATOR of which is a character in the situations and events recounted; a narrative with a HOMODIEGETIC NARRATOR. *Gil Blas, The Great Gatsby, All the King's Men,* and *Kiss Me Deadly* are homodiegetic (as opposed to HETERODIEGETIC) NARRATIVES. ¶Genette 1980, 1983. See also DIEGETIC, EXTRADIEGETIC, FIRST-PERSON NARRATIVE, INTRADIEGETIC, PERSON.

homodiegetic narrator. A NARRATOR who is part of the DIEGESIS (*diégèse*) s/he presents; a narrator who is a character in the situations and events s/he recounts. Gil Blas in the novel by the same name, Jack Burden in *All the King's Men,* and Pablo Ibbieta in "The Wall" are homodiegetic. ¶Genette 1980, 1983; Lanser 1981. See also AUTODIEGETIC NARRATIVE, HETERODIEGETIC NARRATOR, HOMODIEGETIC NARRATIVE, INTRADIEGETIC.

hypodiegetic narrative. See METADIEGETIC NARRATIVE. ¶Bal 1977. Rimmon-Kenan 1983.

I

"I" as protagonist. One of eight possible POINTS OF VIEW according to Friedman's classification. When it is adopted (*Great Expectations, The Catcher in the Rye*), the information provided is limited to the perceptions, feelings, and thoughts of a NARRATOR who is a PROTAGONIST in the situations and events recounted. The latter are then viewed from a fixed center rather than from the periphery. ¶N. Friedman

1955b. See also FIRST-PERSON NARRATIVE, "I" AS WITNESS.

"I" as witness. One of eight possible POINTS OF VIEW according to Friedman's classification. When it is adopted (*Lord Jim, The Great Gatsby*), the information provided is limited to the perceptions, feelings and thoughts of a NARRATOR who is a secondary character in the situations and events recounted. Because the narrator as witness is not a PROTAGONIST, the action is viewed from the periphery rather than from the center. ¶N. Friedman 1955b. See also FIRST-PERSON NARRATIVE, "I" AS PROTAGONIST.

Ich erzählsituation. See FIRST-PERSON NARRATIVE SITUATION. ¶Stanzel 1964, 1971, 1984.

Ich-Form. FIRST-PERSON NARRATIVE form (I-form). ¶Doležel 1973; Füger 1972; Leibfried 1972. See also DU-FORM, ER-FORM.

illocutionary act. An act performed *in* saying something, to accomplish some purpose: in uttering "I promise to be there tomorrow," for instance, I perform the illocutionary act of promising. Along with a LOCUTIONARY ACT and (possibly) a PERLOCUTIONARY ACT, an illocutionary act is involved in the performance of a SPEECH ACT. In the case of so-called indirect speech acts, an illocutionary act is performed indirectly by way of the performance of another illocutionary act: thus, taken literally, "I wish you would open the window" makes an assertion about the addresser's feelings; in particular contexts, however, it can (and does) perform the illocutionary act of making a request. ¶The accomplishment of an illocutionary act depends on the fulfillment of so-called felicity or appropriateness conditions. For example, the conditions for the illocutionary act of asking a question would include the following: (1) the ADDRESSER does not know the answer; (2) s/he believes that the ADDRESSEE may know the answer; (3) s/he wants to know the answer; (4) it is not clear that the addressee will give the answer without being asked. Should (one of) these conditions not be met, the question would be said to be infelicitous or inappropriate (as a question). ¶Among the many attempts to classify illocutionary acts, John Searle's is perhaps the best known: there are representatives (undertaken to represent a state of affairs, e.g., stating, reporting, telling, suggesting, insisting, or swearing that something is the case); directives (undertaken to get an addressee to do something, e.g., requesting, commanding, or pleading); commissives (committing the addresser to doing something, e.g., promising or threatening); expressives (expressing the addresser's psychological attitudes, e.g., thanking, welcoming, or deploring); and declarations (bringing about the state of affairs they refer to, e.g., baptizing, marrying, blessing, or arresting). ¶Viewed as a speech act, one NARRATIVE could therefore be said to involve the illocutionary act of threatening, another one that of deploring, and still another one that of suggesting. More generally, any tellable or reportable narrative could be said to have the illocutionary status of an exclamatory assertion. ¶Austin 1962; Chatman 1978; van Dijk 1977; Lyons 1977; Pratt 1977; Searle 1969, 1975, 1976. See also PERFORMATIVE, REPORTABILITY.

immediate discourse. FREE DIRECT DISCOURSE. With immediate discourse (as opposed to REPORTED DISCOURSE), the character is given the floor without any narratorial introduction, mediation, or patronage (*Les Lauriers sont coupés;* the monologues of Benjy, Quentin, and Jason in the first three sections of *The Sound and the Fury;* Molly Bloom's monologue in *Ulysses*). ¶Genette 1980. See also AUTONOMOUS MONOLOGUE, TYPES OF DISCOURSE.

immediate speech. See IMMEDIATE DISCOURSE. ¶Genette 1980.

impersonal narrator. A maximally COVERT NARRATOR; a narrator with no individuating property other than the fact that he or she is narrating. ¶Ryan 1981. See also ABSENT NARRATOR, NONNARRATED NARRATIVE.

implied author. The AUTHOR'S SECOND SELF, mask, or PERSONA as reconstructed from the text; the implicit image of an author in the text, taken to be standing behind the scenes and to be responsible for its design and for the values and cultural norms it adheres to (Booth). ¶The implied author of a text must be distinguished from its real AUTHOR. In the first place, the same real author (Fielding, Sartre) can write two or more texts, each conveying a different picture of an implied author (*Amelia* and *Joseph Andrews, Nausea* and "Erostratus"). In the second place, one text (having, like all texts, one implied author) can have two or more real authors (*Naked Came the Stranger,* the novels of Ellery Queen, Delly, or Erckmann-Chatrian). ¶The implied author of a narrative text must also be distinguished from the NARRATOR: the former does not recount situations and events (but is taken to be accountable for their selection, distribution, and combination); furthermore, he or she is inferred from the entire text rather than inscribed in it as a teller. Though the distinction can be problematic (e.g., in the case of an ABSENT or maximally COVERT NARRATOR: "The Killers," "Hills Like White Elephants"), it is sometimes very clear (e.g., in the case of many HOMODIEGETIC NARRATIVES: *Great Expectations,* "Haircut"). ¶Bal 1981a; Booth 1983; Bronzwaer 1978; Chatman 1978; Genette 1983.

implied reader. The audience presupposed by a text; a real READER's second self (shaped in accordance with the IMPLIED AUTHOR's values and cultural norms). The implied reader of a text must be distinguished from its real reader. In the first place, the same real reader can read texts presupposing different audiences (and let himself or herself be shaped in accordance with different implied authors' values and norms). In the second place, one text (having, like all texts, one implied reader) can have two or more real readers. ¶The implied reader of a narrative text must also be distinguished from the NARRATEE: the former is the audience of the implied author and is inferrable from the entire text, whereas the latter is the audience of the NARRATOR and is inscribed as such in the text. Though the distinction can be problematic (for example, in the case of a maximally covert narratee: "Hills Like White Elephants"), it is sometimes very clear (for example, in the case of a narrative where the narratee is also a character: Isa, in *Vipers' Tangle*). ¶Booth 1983; Genette 1983; Gibson 1950; Iser 1974, 1978; Rabinowitz 1977.

index. A narrative unit linked to other units in the same SEQUENCE or ACTION in terms other than chronological or causal (say, thematic). Barthes contrasted the index (which implies metaphoric relata) and the FUNCTION (which is metonymically rather than metaphorically related to other units: linked to them in terms of consecution or consequence), and he distinguished two kinds of indices: the index proper (which refers to an atmosphere, a philosophy, a feeling, a personality trait, and signifies implicitly) and the INFORMANT (which provides explicit bits of information about the time and space represented). ¶The same unit can constitute an index and a function. ¶Barthes 1975.

indirect discourse. A TYPE OF DISCOURSE whereby a character's utterances or thoughts are integrated into another utterance or thought (usually but not always) through a back-shift of tenses and a shift from first-person to third-person pronouns. These thoughts or utterances are reported with more or less literal fidelity (as opposed to DIRECT DISCOURSE, where a character's utterances or thoughts are given or quoted in the way the character presumably formulated them): "Mary said: 'I have to go' " becomes "Mary said that she had to go"; " 'I want to take a look at it,' I said" becomes "I said that I wanted to see it"; " 'I have killed my father,' cried out Oedipus" becomes "Oedipus cried out that he had murdered his father." ¶A distinction can be made between "normal," or TAGGED, INDIRECT DISCOURSE (which involves a TAG CLAUSE—"he said that," "she thought that"—introducing and qualifying the represented utterances and thoughts) and FREE

INDIRECT DISCOURSE (which does not and which manifests at least some of the features of the character's ENUNCIATION). ¶Banfield 1982; Chatman 1978; Genette 1980, 1983; Mendilow 1952; Todorov 1981. See also TRANSPOSED DISCOURSE.

indirect speech. INDIRECT DISCOURSE, especially indirect discourse whereby a character's utterances (as opposed to thoughts) are represented. ¶Chatman 1978.

indirect style. See INDIRECT DISCOURSE.

informant. A type of INDEX. As opposed to indices proper (which signify implicitly and refer to an atmosphere, a philosophy, a feeling, a personality trait), informants provide explicit bits of information about the time and space represented. ¶Barthes 1975.

in medias res. The method of starting a narrative (and, more specifically, an epic) with an important situation or event (rather than with the first situation or event in time). Homer opens the *Iliad in medias res* (in the midst of things) rather than *ab ovo* (with an account of Helen's birth, for example). ¶The *in medias res* method is now usually taken to constitute a principle of ordering situations and events (a beginning in the middle of things is followed by a return to an earlier period of time). Originally, however, it referred to a principle of selection (Horace): the narrator starts with the situation pertinent to his or her account (and takes its constituents to be already well-known). ¶Horace 1974; Sternberg 1978.

inquit **formula.** A TAG CLAUSE; a clause appended to the representation of utterances or thoughts, delineating some of their qualities, and identifying the speaker or thinker. In "*Mary said* she was tired" and "How are you? *replied Nancy*," the italicized words constitute *inquit* ("one says") formulas. ¶Bonheim 1982; Chatman 1978; Prince 1978. See also ATTRIBUTIVE DISCOURSE, VERBUM DICENDI.

inside view. The representation of a character's mind. ¶Booth 1983. See also AUTHORITY.

intercalated narration. A type of NARRATION whereby a NARRATING INSTANCE is temporally situated between two moments of the ACTION; an INTERPOLATED NARRATING. Intercalated narration is characteristic of epistolary narratives (*Pamela*) and diary narratives (*Doctor Glas, Diary of a Country Priest*). ¶Genette 1980; Prince 1982.

intercalation. See EMBEDDING. ¶Greimas and Courtés 1982.

interest point of view. The consideration of narrated situations and events in terms of the character's interests they (most) evoke and concern. In "Though he didn't realize it, these developments were disastrous for John," the interest point of view is John's. ¶Chatman 1978.

interior monologue. The nonmediated presentation of a character's thoughts and impressions or perceptions; an extended stretch of FREE DIRECT THOUGHT (*Les Lauriers sont coupés,* Molly Bloom's monologue in *Ulysses*). ¶Interior monologue (*monologue intérieur, stiller Monolog*) is now frequently taken to subsume STREAM OF CONSCIOUSNESS as a particular variant. However, it has sometimes been opposed to stream of consciousness: interior monologue would present a character's thoughts rather than impressions or perceptions, and stream of consciousness would present both impressions and thoughts; or else, the former would respect morphology and syntax, whereas the latter would not and would thus capture thought in its nascent stage, prior to any logical organization. On the other hand, the two terms have often been used interchangeably; in fact, Dujardin—whose *Les Lauriers sont coupés* probably constitutes the most famous example of a text written entirely in FREE DIRECT DISCOURSE—stressed stylistic criteria and effects associated with stream of consciousness in his definition of interior monologue. ¶Bickerton 1967; Bowling 1950; Chatman 1978; Cohn 1978, 1981; Dujardin 1931; Francoeur 1976; M. Friedman 1955; Genette 1980; Humphrey 1954; Scholes and Kellogg 1966. See also AUTONOMOUS MONOLOGUE, DRAMATIC MONOLOGUE, TYPES OF DISCOURSE.

internal action. What characters think and feel as opposed to what they say and do (EXTERNAL ACTION). ¶Brooks and Warren 1959.

internal analysis. A narrator's account, in his or her own words, of a character's thoughts and impressions; a NARRATIVE REPORT of thoughts and impressions in words that are recognizably the narrator's (as opposed to NARRATED MONOLOGUE); a PSYCHONARRATION. ¶Bowling 1950; Chatman 1978; Cohn 1978. See also ANALYSIS.

internal focalization. A type of FOCALIZATION whereby information is conveyed in terms of a character's (conceptual or perceptual) POINT OF VIEW or PERSPECTIVE.

¶Internal focalization can be fixed (when one and only one perspective is adopted: *The Ambassadors, What Maisie Knew,* Robert Montgomery's *The Lady in the Lake*), variable (when different perspectives are adopted in turn to present different situations and events: *The Age of Reason, The Golden Bowl*), or multiple (when the same situations and events are presented more than once, each time in terms of a different perspective: *The Ring and the Book, The Moonstone, Rashomon*). ¶Bal 1985; Genette 1980. See also FIXED INTERNAL FOCALIZATION, INTERNAL POINT OF VIEW, MULTIPLE INTERNAL FOCALIZATION, PERSONAL NARRATIVE SITUATION, VARIABLE INTERNAL FOCALIZATION, VISION.

internal plot. A PLOT focusing on internal feelings and movements, as in psychological novels. ¶H. James 1972. See also EXTERNAL PLOT.

internal point of view. See INTERNAL FOCALIZATION. ¶Prince 1982; Uspenskij 1973.

interpolated narrating. See INTERCALATED NARRATION. ¶Genette 1980.

interspersed narration. See INTERCALATED NARRATION. ¶Lanser 1981.

intertext. 1. A text (or set of texts) that is cited, rewritten, prolonged, or generally transformed by another text and that makes the latter meaningful. Homer's *Odyssey* is one of the intertexts of Joyce's *Ulysses,* and INTERTEXTUALITY obtains between the two. ¶In Riffaterre's influential view, a text and its intertext are homologous, and the latter leaves in the former traces controlling its decipherment. 2. A text insofar as it absorbs and binds together a multiplicity of other texts (Jenny).

In this acceptation, Joyce's *Ulysses* would be the intertext absorbing such texts as Homer's *Odyssey.* More generally, any text could be taken to constitute an intertext. **3.** A set of texts that are intertextually linked (Arrivé): given that intertextuality obtains between Homer's *Odyssey* and Joyce's *Ulysses,* the two texts would be said to constitute an intertext. ¶Arrivé 1973; Barthes 1981b; Jenny 1982; Morgan 1985; Riffaterre 1978, 1980, 1983.

intertextuality. The relation(s) obtaining between a given text and other texts which it cites, rewrites, absorbs, prolongs, or generally transforms and in terms of which it is intelligible. ¶The notion of intertextuality was formulated and developed by Kristeva (inspired by Bakhtin). In its most restricted acceptation (Genette), the term designates the relation(s) between one text and other ones which are demonstrably present in it. In its most general and radical acceptation (Barthes, Kristeva), the term designates the relations between any text (in the broad sense of signifying matter) and the sum of knowledge, the potentially infinite network of codes and signifying practices that allows it to have meaning. ¶Barthes 1981b; Culler 1981; Genette 1982; Jenny 1982; Kristeva 1969, 1984; Morgan 1985; Ricardou 1971; Riffaterre 1978, 1980, 1983. See also INTERTEXT.

interweaving. See ALTERNATION. ¶Ducrot and Todorov 1979.

intradiegetic. DIEGETIC; pertaining to or part of the DIEGESIS (*diégèse*) presented (in a PRIMARY NARRATIVE) by an EXTRADIEGETIC narrator. In *Père Goriot,* for example, Rastignac is intradiegetic. Similarly, in *Manon Lescaut,* M. de Renoncourt, the extradiegetic narrator of the primary narrative, is intradiegetic insofar as he functions as a character in the diegesis he presents; and Des Grieux is intradiegetic as a character in M. de Renoncourt's narrative (and META-DIEGETIC as a character in his own narrative). ¶An intradiegetic narrator is not equivalent to a HOMODIEGETIC one. Thus, in *Arabian Nights,* Scheherazade functions as a HETERODIEGETIC NARRATOR (since she does not tell her own story) and as an intradiegetic rather than extradiegetic one (since she is a character in a framing narrative that she does not tell). Conversely, in *Gil Blas,* the narrator is a homodiegetic and extradiegetic one (he tells his own story, but as a narrator, he is not part of any diegesis). ¶Genette 1980, 1983; Lanser 1981; Rimmon 1976. See also DIEGETIC LEVEL.

intrigue. The PLOT; the aggregate of motifs characterizing the characters' machinations, conflicts, and struggles. ¶Tomashevsky 1965.

intrusive narrator. A NARRATOR commenting in his or her own voice on the situations and events presented, their presentation, or its context; a narrator relying on and characterized by commentarial excursuses or intrusions (*Eugénie Grandet, Barchester Towers, Tom Jones*). ¶Blin 1954; Genette 1980; Prince 1982. See also AUTHOR'S INTRUSION, COMMENTARY, OVERT NARRATOR.

inverted content. The thematic situation whose TRANSFORMATION into a contrary (or contradictory) situation marks the completion of a narrative SEQUENCE. ¶Narrative can be viewed as correlating a temporal opposition (before/after, initial situation/final situation) and a thematic one (inverted content/RESOLVED CONTENT). ¶Chabrol 1973; Greimas 1970; Rastier 1973.

isochrony. **1.** The steadiness of narrative SPEED. An isochronous narrative is one the speed of which is constant, as in "Susan wrote for an hour, then she drank for an hour, then she slept for an hour." **2.** The equality between the duration of a situation or event and the duration of its representation. ¶Bal 1985; Genette 1980. See also ANISOCHRONY, DURATION.

isodiegetic. Part of the same DIEGESIS (*diégèse*). In *Nausea,* the Self-Taught Man and Anny are isodiegetic; in *Heart of Darkness,* Marlow's mates on the *Nellie* and Kurz are not. ¶Genette 1980. See also DIEGETIC.

isotopy. The repetition of semiotic features that institutes the coherence of a text. In "Everybody was beautifully dressed. John and Mary were led to a magnificent table in the middle of a splendidly decorated room and were offered champagne," the clustering of terms capable of evoking luxury—"beautifully dressed," "magnificent," "splendidly decorated," "champagne"—can be said to constitute a "luxury" isotopy. ¶In its more restricted acceptation, the term is taken to designate the repetition of semantic units in a text (or part thereof). In its broadest sense, its designates the repetition of units at any and all textual levels (phonetic, stylistic, rhetorical, syntactic, prosodic, etc). ¶Adam 1985; Eco 1979, 1984; Greimas 1983b; Greimas and Courtés 1982; Rastier 1973.

iterative narrative. A narrative or part thereof with a FREQUENCY whereby what happens *n* times is recounted once: "Every Sunday, we went to the beach." An iterative narrative (or iterative series) can have a DETERMINATION (the span of time in which an event or set of events is said to recur), a SPECIFICATION (the rhythm of recurrence of the event or set of events), and an EXTENSION (the duration of the recurring event or set of events). In "During a period of eight weeks, I ran once a week for an hour," the series has a determination of eight weeks, a specification of one day out of seven, and an extension of one hour. ¶Genette 1980.

joining. The connecting of two TRIADS each of which presents the same process but considers it from a different point of view (say, that of the protagonist in the first and that of the antagonist in the second) and thus constitutes a different set of FUNCTIONS. ¶Bremond 1973, 1980.

junction. A relation linking the SUBJECT and the OBJECT and yielding STASIS STATEMENTS. There are two basic types of junction: CONJUNCTION ("X is with Y," "X has Y") and DISJUNCTION ("X is not with Y," "X does not have Y"). ¶Greimas and Courtés 1982; Hénault 1983.

K

kernel. A BOUND MOTIF; a CARDINAL FUNCTION; a NUCLEUS (*noyau*). As opposed to SATELLITES, kernels are logically essential to the narrative action and cannot be eliminated without destroying its causal-chronological coherence. ¶Barthes 1975; Chatman 1978.

L

langue. The language system or CODE governing the production (and reception) of individual utterances (PAROLE) in a given language. According to Saussure, who articulated the distinction, *langue* rather than *parole* constitutes the main object of linguistic study. By analogy with (Saussurean) linguistics, NARRATOLOGY attempts to characterize "narrative *langue*" (the code or set of principles governing the production of all and only narratives) rather than to study individual narratives (equivalent to *parole*). ¶Saussure 1966. See also NARRATIVE COMPETENCE.

laying bare. Calling attention to a device, technique, or convention. According to Tomashevsky and the Russian Formalists, laying bare a device, or BARING THE DEVICE (as opposed to MOTIVATION), underlines the convention-governed character of a text, its fictionality, its literary nature. ¶Ducrot and Todorov 1979; Lemon and Reis 1965;

Shklovsky 1965b; Tomashevsky 1965.

leitmotif. A frequently recurring MOTIF, related to and expressive of a character, situation, or event. Vinteuil's little phrase in *Remembrance of Things Past* functions as a leitmotif. ¶The term was originally used in connection with Wagnerian music. ¶Ducrot and Todorov 1979; Tomashevsky 1965.

lexia. A textual unit or unit of reading of variable dimension constituting the best space in which meaning can be observed. ¶Barthes 1974.

limited point of view. A FOCALIZATION or POINT OF VIEW that is subject to conceptual or perceptual constraints (as opposed to OMNISCIENT POINT OV VIEW). *The Ambassadors* is told in terms of a limited point of view, and so is "Bliss." ¶N. Friedman 1955b; Stanzel 1984.

linking. A combination of narrative SEQUENCES (recounted in the same NARRATING INSTANCE or in different ones) such that one sequence is conjoined with (placed after) another or such that the end of one sequence constitutes the beginning of another. A narrative like "John was happy, then he got divorced, then he became unhappy and Mary was unhappy, then she got married, then she became happy" can be said to result from the linking of "John was happy, then he got divorced, then he became unhappy" and "Mary was unhappy, then she got married, then she became happy." Similarly, a narrative like "She was in good health, then she ate a rotten apple, then she became ill, then she took some medicine, then she felt very well" can be said to result from the linking of "She was in good health, then she ate a rotten apple, then she became ill" and "She became ill, then she took some medicine, then she felt very well." ¶Along with EMBEDDING and ALTERNATION, linking, or CONJOINING, is one of the basic ways of combining narrative sequences. ¶Bremond 1973; Ducrot and Todorov 1979; Prince 1973, 1982; Todorov 1966, 1981. See also COMPLEX STORY, ENCHAINMENT, TRIAD.

lion. One of six FUNCTIONS or fundamental ROLES isolated by Souriau (in his study of the possibilities of drama). The Lion (analogous to Greimas's SUBJECT and Propp's HERO) is the force oriented in terms of the SUN (or OBJECT) and works for the benefit of the EARTH (or RECEIVER). ¶Scholes 1974; Souriau 1950. See also ACTANT.

locutionary act. An act of saying, of producing a grammatical utterance. When I say "The earth is round," for instance, I perform the locutionary act of making a sentence in accordance with the rules of English. Along with an ILLOCUTIONARY ACT and (possibly) a PERLOCUTIONARY ACT, a locutionary act is involved in the performance of a SPEECH ACT. ¶Austin 1962; Lyons 1977; Searle 1969.

logos. Subject matter; topic; thought; argument. For Aristotle, the imitation of a real action, or PRAXIS, constitutes an argument, or *logos,* providing the basis for the MYTHOS, or PLOT. ¶The distinction between *logos* and *mythos* is suggestive of that between STORY and DISCOURSE or FABULA and SJUŽET. ¶Aristotle 1968; Chatman 1978.

M

macrostructure. The abstract underlying structure of a text; the DEEP STRUCTURE of a text defining its global meaning. The macrostructure is converted into the MICROSTRUCTURE (or SURFACE STRUCTURE) by a set of operations or TRANSFORMATIONS. ¶Van Dijk 1972, 1974–75, 1976a. See also NARRATIVE GRAMMAR.

main narrator. The NARRATOR introducing the entire narrative (including all the mini-narratives composing it or parts of it); the narrator ultimately responsible for the whole narrative (including title, epigraphs, etc.) ¶Prince 1982.

main test. See DECISIVE TEST.

manifestation. The SUBSTANCE of the DISCOURSE or of the EXPRESSION plane of narrative (as opposed to its FORM); the medium (verbal, cinematic, balletic, etc.) of narrative representation. A cinematic representation of a man eating, then sleeping and a verbal representation of it can constitute two different manifestations of the same form of the discourse (or set of NARRATIVE STATEMENTS). ¶Chatman 1978. See also NARRATIVE MEDIUM.

manipulation. In the Greimassian account of canonical narrative structure, the action of the SENDER on the SUBJECT to make the latter execute a given program. ¶Adam 1984, 1985; Greimas 1983a; Greimas and Courtés 1982. See also CONTRACT, NARRATIVE SCHEMA, SANCTION.

Mars. One of six FUNCTIONS or fundamental ROLES isolated by Souriau (in his study of the possibilities of drama). Mars (analogous to Greimas's OPPONENT and Propp's VILLAIN and FALSE HERO) is the ANTAGONIST, or enemy, of the LION. ¶Scholes 1974; Souriau 1950. See also ACTANT, ANTISUBJECT.

mask. A CHARACTERIZATION device whereby the physical features (and/or clothes, furnishings, names, etc.) of a character are in harmony with his or her personality. ¶Tomashevsky 1965.

mediated narration. A narration in which the narrator's presence makes itself felt; a narration featuring an OVERT rather than COVERT NARRATOR; a narration in which DIEGESIS, TELLING, or recounting, rather than MIMESIS, SHOWING, or enacting, are dominant. ¶Chatman 1978. See also ABSENT NARRATOR.

mediation. The process or operation effected by a MEDIATOR and correlating (initial and final sets of) situations in myth and narrative; the intratextual TRANSFORMATION linking two (sets of opposite) situations. ¶Lévi-Strauss 1963; Köngäs-Maranda and Maranda 1962.

mediator. The ACTOR or character through whom a MEDIATION is effected. The mediator is, at first, linked to actions in opposition to the antagonist but then proves capable of engaging in the same (kind of) actions undertaken by that antagonist.

message. One of the fundamental constituents of any act of (verbal) communication. The message is the text (the signifying material, the set of signs to be decoded) sent by the ADDRESSER to the ADDRESSEE. ¶Jakobson 1960. See also CODE, CONSTITUTIVE FACTORS OF COMMUNICATION, POETIC FUNCTION.

metadiegetic. Pertaining to or part of a DIEGESIS (*diégèse*) that is embedded in another one and, more particularly, in that of the PRIMARY NARRATIVE. ¶Genette 1980, 1983. See also DIEGETIC LEVEL, METADIEGETIC NARRATIVE.

metadiegetic narrative. A narrative embedded within another narrative and, more particularly, within the PRIMARY NARRATIVE; a HYPODIEGETIC NARRATIVE. The situations and events recounted by Des Grieux in *Manon Lescaut* are METADIEGETIC in relation to those recounted by M. de Renoncourt (which are DIEGETIC or INTRADIEGETIC). ¶When a metadiegetic narrative functions as a diegetic one (when its metadiegetic status is forgotten, as it were), it is said to be a PSEUDO-DIEGETIC NARRATIVE (the *Theaetetus*). ¶Genette 1980, 1983. See also DIEGETIC LEVEL, EMBEDDING.

metalanguage. A (natural or artificial) language used to describe another language (the object language). For example, the language used by grammarians to describe the functioning of English is a metalanguage. ¶By extension, any language used to describe a given domain constitutes a metalanguage: NARRATIVE GRAMMAR can be considered to be the metalanguage characterizing the form and functioning of narrative. ¶Lyons 1977.

metalepsis. The intrusion into one DIEGESIS (*diégèse*) of a being from another diegesis; the mingling of two distinct DIEGETIC LEVELS. Should an EXTRADIEGETIC narrator suddenly enter the world of the situations and events recounted, for instance, a metalepsis obtains. ¶Genette 1980, 1983.

metalingual function. One of the FUNCTIONS OF COMMUNICATION in terms of which any communicative (verbal) act may be structured and oriented; the METALINGUISTIC FUNCTION. When the communicative act is centered on the CODE (rather than on one of the other CONSTITUTIVE FACTORS OF COMMUNICATION), it (mainly) has a metalingual function. More specifically, those passages in a narrative focusing on and explaining the language constituting it can be said to fulfill a metalingual function: "In Anjou, the *frippe,* a colloquial word, designates what goes with bread, from butter spread on toast—the commonest kind—to peach preserves, the most distinguished of all the *frippes.*" ¶Jakobson 1960; Prince 1982.

metalinguistic function. See METALINGUAL FUNCTION.

metanarrative. About narrative; describing narrative. A narrative having (a) narrative as (one of) its topic(s) is (a) metanarrative. More specifically, a narrative referring to itself and to those elements by which it is constituted and communicated, a narrative discussing itself, a SELF-REFLEXIVE NARRATIVE, is metanarrative. Even more specifically, the passages or units in a narrative that refer explicitly to the CODES or subcodes in terms of which the narrative signifies are metanarrative and constitute METANARRATIVE SIGNS. ¶Hamon 1977; Hutcheon 1984; Prince 1982. See also NARRATIVE CODE.

metanarrative sign. In a narrative, a sign explicitly referring to (one of) the CODES (or one of the subcodes) in terms of which the narrative signifies; a sign predicated on another sign considered as an element in the code framing the narrative in which they both appear. ¶The metanarrative sign explicitly comments on a narrative unit *x* and provides an answer to such questions as "What does *x* mean in the (sub-)code according to which the narrative is developed?," "What is *x* in the (sub-)code used?," or "How does *x* function in the (sub-)code according to which the narrative can be understood?" In "John punched Jim, and Jim punched him back. This fight only lasted a few seconds," for example, "this fight" constitutes a metanarrative sign and, more specifically, a metaproairetic one: it explicitly comments on the meaning of "John punched Jim, and Jim punched him back" in terms of a PROAIRETIC CODE. ¶Prince 1977, 1982. See also METANARRATIVE, NARRATIVE CODE.

metaphor. A figure of speech through which a term designating a notion, A, is substituted for or identified with another term designating another notion, B, thereby ascribing to B one or more of the qualities of A or investing it with qualities associated with A (consider "A woman is a rose" where "rose" is identified with "woman" or "The winter of my life is fast approaching" where "winter" is substituted for something like "final part"). ¶Jakobson argued in an important essay that two processes stand at the heart of verbal activity: the metaphorical process, where one discourse topic leads to another through relations of similarity (involving selection and substitution), and the metonymical process, where one discourse topic leads to another through relations of contiguity. Following and expanding Jakobson, who emphasized the importance of the metonymical process in realistic fiction, narratologists have tended to treat NARRATIVE as primarily metonymic: they have argued that MOTIFS and FUNCTIONS are integrated into SEQUENCES mainly through relations of contiguity. Yet it can also be argued that narrative is—in an important way—a function of the metaphoric process: in a narrative sequence, the last situation or event constitutes a partial repetition of the first; in other words, there is a relation of similarity between the two. ¶Culler 1981; Jakobson 1956; Lodge 1977. See also METONYMY, TRANSFORMATION.

metonymy. A figure of speech whereby a term designating a notion, A, is used for another term designating another notion, B, related to A as cause and effect, container and thing contained, or part and whole (consider "In the sweat of thy face shalt thou eat bread" where "sweat" as effect is substituted for "labor" as cause, or "She smoked a whole pack" where "pack" as container is substituted for "cigarettes" as thing contained). ¶In an influential essay, Jakobson argued that two processes stand at the heart of verbal activity: the metonymical process, where one discourse topic leads to another through relations of contiguity (involving CAUSALITY and inclusion), and the metaphorical process, where one discourse topic leads to another through relations of similarity. Following and expanding Jakobson, who emphasized the importance of the metonymical process in realistic fiction (the narrator often digresses metonymically from CHARACTER to SETTING and from plot to atmosphere), many narratologists have treated NARRATIVE as predominantly metonymic. Specifically, they have argued that MOTIFS

and FUNCTIONS are integrated into SEQUENCES primarily through relations of contiguity (the narrated situations and events constitute logico-temporal chains). ¶Culler 1981; Jakobson 1956; Lodge 1977. See also METAPHOR.

microstructure. The SURFACE STRUCTURE of a text; the particular way the MACROSTRUCTURE (or DEEP STRUCTURE) of a text is realized. The microstructure is related to the macrostructure by a set of operations, or TRANSFORMATIONS. ¶Van Dijk 1972, 1974–75, 1976a. See also NARRATIVE GRAMMAR.

middle. The set of incidents in a PLOT or ACTION between the BEGINNING and the END. The middle follows and is followed by other incidents. ¶Students of narrative have pointed out that the middle is doubly oriented (prospectively from beginning to end and retrospectively from end to beginning), that it paradoxically progresses toward the end while, at the same time, postponing the reaching of the end, and that it constitutes a (more or less prolonged) situation of deviance from the "normal" (the non-NARRATABLE). ¶Aristotle 1968; Brooks 1984. See also COMPLICATING ACTION, COMPLICATION, NARRATIVITY, RAVELLING.

mimesis. In narratology, SHOWING, enacting (as opposed to TELLING, recounting). ¶Plato distinguished between two poetic modes: with mimesis (imitation), the poet delivers a speech as if s/he were someone else (a given character), whereas with DIEGESIS (narration, *diégésis*), the poet delivers a speech in his or her own name. While mimesis therefore involves no (or minimal) narratorial mediation, such mediation is characteristic of diegesis. For Aristotle, according to whom all art is imitation and the various arts differ depending on object, means, and manner or mode, the two modes as well as the so-called mixed mode (which is formed of the other two and illustrated by Homer, for example) constitute three varieties of mimesis. In Aristotelian terms, verbal narrative could then be characterized as the imitation of an action (*mimēsis praxeōs*), using linguistic means and adopting any one of the three modes. ¶In a discussion of Aristotle's *Poetics* and its pertinence for understanding narrative, Ricoeur develops a threefold model of mimesis as imitation whereby PLOT, which provides the means that allow us to grasp and make sense of human time, is viewed as a temporal configuration mediating between the time prefigured in the practical field (the field of life and human action) and the time refigured through the reception of the narrative. ¶Perhaps no concept has exerted a more powerful influence than imitation in the Western critico-literary tradition, whether through encouraging the accurate representation of life or through fostering the imitation of classic works and ancient masters or—most generally—through promoting the view that the work of art, by holding a mirror up to nature (and not merely being a mirror itself), reveals the presence of the generic in the specific, the universal in the particular, the essential in the phenomenal. ¶Aristotle 1968; Frye 1957; Genette 1980; Plato 1968; Ricoeur 1984, 1985. See also NARRATIVE.

minimal narrative. **1.** A NARRATIVE representing only a single EVENT: "She opened the door." **2.** A narrative containing a single TEMPORAL JUNCTURE (Labov): "She ate then she slept." ¶Genette 1983; Labov 1972. See also COMPLEX STORY, MINIMAL STORY.

minimal story. A narrative recounting only two STATES and one EVENT such that (1) one state precedes the event in time and the event precedes the other state in time (and causes it); (2) the second state constitutes the inverse (or the modification, including the "zero" modification) of the first. "John was happy, then he saw Peter, then, as a result, he was unhappy" is a minimal story. ¶Prince 1973. See also COMPLEX STORY, MINIMAL NARRATIVE, PROCESS, STORY.

mise en abyme. A miniature replica of a text embedded within that text; a textual part reduplicating, reflecting, or mirroring (one or more than one aspect of) the textual whole. In *The Counterfeiters,* Edouard's writing of a novel entitled *The Counterfeiters* constitutes a *mise en abyme.* ¶The term comes from heraldry: a figure in an escutcheon is said to be *en abyme* when it constitutes a miniature of that escutcheon. ¶Dällenbach 1977.

modality. The qualification of a statement or set of statements by a modal operator (cf. "John was sick" and "John did not know that he was sick"). The operator may, for example, be alethic (express the modalities of possibility, impossibility, and necessity), deontic (express the modalities of permission, prohibition, and obligation), axiological (express the modalities of goodness, badness, and indifference), or epistemic (express the modalities of knowledge, ignorance, and belief). ¶Various modal constraints govern NARRATIVE DOMAINS and, more generally, determine what "happens" in a narrative by establishing what is or could be the case in the world represented, regulating the characters' knowledge, setting their values, obligations, and goals, and in general guiding their course of action. Indeed, it has been argued that narratives develop along modal axes and represent transitions from certain states on these axes to other ones (going, for example, from what has to be done to what can be done; from what is bad to what is good; and/or from what is not known to what is known). ¶In the Greimassian model of narrative, modalizations along the axes of ability (being able to do or be), desire (wanting to do or be), knowledge (knowing how to do or be), and obligation (having to do or be) are the most important. ¶Doležel 1976; Greimas 1970, 1971; Greimas and Courtés 1982; Pavel 1980, 1985; Ryan 1985. See also ACTANTIAL ROLE, ATOMIC STORY, COMPETENCE.

mode. 1. DISTANCE. The extent of narratorial mediation characterizes the mode of a narrative: SHOWING and TELLING are two different modes. ¶Along with PERSPECTIVE or POINT OF VIEW, mode constitutes the category of narrative MOOD. 2. A fictional world considered from the point of view of the hero's power of action in relation to human beings and to their environment. Frye argues that the hero can be superior, equal, or inferior in kind or in degree to others and/or to the environment and he characterizes five modes: (1) myth (supe-rior in kind to both); (2) romance (superior in degree to both); (3) high mimesis (superior in degree to others but not to the environment); (4) low mimesis (equal to both others and the environment); (5) irony (inferior to others or to the environment). ¶Frye 1957; Todorov 1966, 1981.

molecular story. A story consisting of two or more ATOMIC STORIES; a COMPOUND STORY. ¶Doležel 1976. See also MODALITY.

monologic narrative. A narrative characterized by a unifying voice or consciousness superior to other voices or consciousnesses in that narrative (*Eugénie Grandet, A Tale of Two Cities*). In monologic as opposed to DIALOGIC NARRATIVE, the narrator's views, judgments, and knowledge constitute the ultimate authority with respect to the world represented. ¶Bakhtin 1981, 1984; Pascal 1977.

monologue. A long discourse produced by one character (and not addressed to other characters). Should the monologue be unspoken (should it consist of the character's verbalized thoughts), it constitutes an INTERIOR MONOLOGUE. Should it be spoken, it constitutes an exterior monologue or soliloquy. ¶Holman 1972. See also DIALOGUE.

montage. A technique whereby the meaning of a given series of situations and events comes from their juxtaposition rather than from their constituent features (cf. the "Newsreels" in Dos Passos's *U.S.A.*). The term is particularly associated with motion pictures. ¶Metz 1974; Souvage 1965.

mood. The set of modalities—namely, DISTANCE or MODE and PERSPECTIVE or POINT OF VIEW—regulating narrative information. The mood of a narrative will vary depending on whether SHOWING or TELLING is in evidence, for example; it will also vary depending on whether INTERNAL or EXTERNAL FOCALIZATION is adopted. ¶Genette 1980.

moon. One of six fundamental ROLES or FUNCTIONS isolated by Souriau (in his study of the possibilities of drama). The Moon (analogous to Propp's DONOR and HELPER as well as to Greimas's HELPER) assists the LION or HERO. ¶Scholes 1974; Souriau 1950. See also ACTANT.

motif. **1.** A minimal thematic unit. When a motif recurs frequently in a given text, it is called a LEITMOTIF. ¶A motif should not be confused with a THEME, which constitutes a more abstract and more general semantic unit manifested by or reconstructed from a set of motifs: if glasses are a motif in *Princess Brambilla,* vision is a theme in that work. A motif should also be distinguished from a TOPOS, which is a specific complex of motifs that frequently appears in (literary) texts (the wise fool, the aged child, the *locus amoenus,* etc.) **2.** A minimal narrative unit at the syntactic level; a NARRATIVE STATEMENT. For Tomashevsky, motifs can be static (designate a STATE) or dynamic (designate an EVENT). Furthermore, they can be logically essential to the narrative action and its causal-chronological coherence (BOUND MOTIFS), or they can be logically inessential to it (FREE MOTIFS). **3.** An element fulfilling or manifesting a MOTIFEME. A motif is to a motifeme as a phone (a sound of language) is to a phoneme (a distinctive sound class), a morph to a morpheme, or an ACTION to a FUNCTION. ¶Bremond 1982; Daemmrich and Daemmrich 1986; Ducrot and Todorov 1979;

Dundes 1964; Tomashevsky 1965. See also ALLOMOTIF.

motifeme. A FUNCTION (in the Proppian sense). Dundes, who borrowed the term from Pike, suggested its adoption to designate the fundamental structural unit of a folktale: a motifeme is specified or manifested by a MOTIF and is to the latter as a function is to an ACTION, a phoneme to a phone, or a morpheme to a morph. ¶Doležel 1972; Dundes 1964; Pike 1967.

motivation. **1.** The network of devices justifying the introduction of a MOTIF, a complex of motifs, or, more generally, a constituent feature of a (literary) text; the reason for the use of a given textual element; COMPOSITION. ¶Tomashevsky distinguished between compositional motivation (referring to the usefulness of the motif), realistic motivation (stressing the lifelikeness, realism, or authenticity of the motif), and artistic motivation (justifying the introduction of the motif in terms of the requirements of "art"). **2.** The complex of circumstances, reasons, purposes, and impulses governing a character's actions (and making them plausible). ¶Brooks and Warren 1959; Ducrot and Todorov 1979; Genette 1968; Propp 1968; Rimmon-Kenan 1983; Tomashevsky 1965; Wellek and Warren 1949. See also LAYING BARE, NATURALIZATION, VERISIMILITUDE.

move. **1.** Any sequence of FUNCTIONS proceeding from a Villainy or a Lack to a DENOUEMENT. According to Propp, every tale (*skázka*) consists of one or more moves. ¶Moves can be combined through EMBEDDING, ALTERNATION, and LINKING, or CONJOINING. **2.** A CARDINAL FUNCTION; a

NUCLEUS; a NARREME. In Pavel's NARRATIVE GRAMMAR, a Move is an action called for by a Problem (e.g. "John's life was threatened"), representing an effort toward its Solution (e.g., "John left the country"), and bringing about another Move or the end of the story. ¶Pavel 1985; Propp 1968. See also NARRATIVE DOMAIN.

multiple internal focalization. A type of INTERNAL FOCALIZATION or POINT OF VIEW whereby the same situations and events are presented more than once, each time in terms of a different focalizer (*The Ring and the Book, The Moonstone, Rashomon*). ¶Genette 1980. See also FOCALIZATION.

multiple internal point of view. See MULTIPLE INTERNAL FOCALIZATION. ¶Prince 1982.

multiple selective omniscience. One of eight possible POINTS OF VIEW according to Friedman's classification: multiple selective omniscience characterizes the HETERODIEGETIC NARRATOR adopting VARIABLE INTERNAL FOCALIZATION (*To the Lighthouse*). ¶N. Friedman 1955b. See also SELECTIVE OMNISCIENCE.

myth. A traditional narrative, usually associated with religious belief and ritual, that expresses and justifies an exemplary aspect of the way things are. ¶According to Lévi-Strauss, the structure of myth can be expressed through a four-term homology relating two pairs of opposite MYTHEMES (*A* and *B; C* and *D*): $A:B::C:D$ (*A* is to *B* as *C* is to *D*). This formula presumably accounts for the meaning of myth, whereby one kind of irreconcilability (contradiction, opposition) is made simpler to contend with through being related to another, more

common kind. Thus, the Oedipus myth relates the opposition non-autochtonous origin of man / autochtonous origin of man, to the more acceptable opposition overestimation of kinship ties / underestimation of kinship ties. ¶Frye 1957; Greimas 1970; Jolles 1956; Lévi-Strauss 1963, 1965–71; Scholes and Kellogg 1966.

mytheme. The fundamental constituent unit of MYTH. ¶Lévi-Strauss 1963.

mythos. A PLOT, an arrangement of incidents. For Aristotle, *mythos* consists in the selection and possible rearrangement of the units constituting LOGOS (the imitation of a real action, or PRAXIS). ¶The distinction between *mythos* and *logos* is suggestive of that between DISCOURSE and STORY or SJUŽET and FABULA. ¶Aristotle 1968; Chatman 1978. See also THOUGHT.

narratable. That which is worthy of being told; that which is susceptible of or calls for narration. ¶Brooks 1984; Miller 1981. See also MIDDLE, REPORTABILITY.

narrated. **1.** The set of situations and events recounted in a narrative; the STORY (as opposed to the DISCOURSE). **2.** The signs in a narrative representing the situations and events narrated (as opposed to the NARRATING). ¶Prince 1982.

narrated monologue. FREE INDIRECT DISCOURSE in the context of THIRD-PERSON NARRATIVE. With narrated monologue (as opposed to PSYCHONARRATION), the account of the character's discourse is mainly in words that are recognizably the character's. ¶Cohn 1966, 1978. See also QUOTED MONOLOGUE, SELF-NARRATED MONOLOGUE.

narratee. The one who is narrated to, as inscribed in the text. There is at least one (more or less overtly represented) narratee per narrative, located at the same DIEGETIC LEVEL as the NARRATOR addressing him or her. In a given narrative, there may, of course, be several different narratees, each addressed in turn by the same narrator (*Vipers' Tangle*) or by a different one (*The Immoralist*). ¶Like the narrator, the narratee may be represented as a character, playing a more or less important role in the situations and events recounted (*Vipers' Tangle, The Immoralist, Heart of Darkness, A Change of Heart*). Very often, however, the narratee is not represented as a character (*Tom Jones, Eugénie Grandet, Crime and Punishment*). ¶The narratee— a purely textual construct—must be distinguished from the real READER or RECEIVER. After all, the same real reader can read different narratives (each having different narratees); and the same narrative (which always has the same set of narratees) can have an indefinitely varying set of real readers. ¶The narratee must also be distinguished from the IMPLIED READER: the former constitutes the narrator's audience and is inscribed as such in the text; the latter constitutes the IMPLIED AUTHOR's audience (and is inferable from the entire text). Though the distinction can be problematic (for example, in the case of a maximally covert narratee: "Hills Like White Elephants"), it is sometimes very clear (for example, in the case of a narrative where the narratee is also a character: Isa, in *Vipers' Tangle*). ¶Genette 1980, 1983; Mosher 1980; Piwowarczyk 1976; Prince 1980, 1982. See also DISTANCE, NARRATING INSTANCE, PERSON.

narrating. 1. The telling or relating of one or more events. 2. The DISCOURSE (as opposed to the STORY). 3. The signs in a narrative representing the narrating activity, its origin, its destination, and its context (as opposed to the NARRATED). ¶Genette 1980; Prince 1982. See also INTERPOLATED NARRATING, PRIOR NARRATING, SIMULTANEOUS NARRATING, SUBSEQUENT NARRATING.

narrating instance. The act of recounting a series of situations and events and, by extension, the spatio-temporal context (including the NARRATOR and the NARRATEE) of that act. ¶There can be several distinct narrating instances in a single narrative, each involving the same narrator (*Vipers' Tangle, Diary of a Superfluous Man, Doctor Glas*) or a different one (*The Immoralist, Manon Lescaut*). ¶Genette 1980, 1983. See also PRIMARY NARRATIVE, VOICE.

narration. 1. A NARRATIVE; a discourse representing one or more events. Narration is traditionally distinguished from DESCRIPTION and from COMMENTARY but usually incorporates them within itself. 2. The production of a narrative; the recounting of a series of situations and events. A POSTERIOR NARRATION follows the narrated situations and events in time (and is characteristic of "classical" or "traditional" narrative); an ANTERIOR NARRATION precedes them in time (as in PREDICTIVE

NARRATIVE); a SIMULTANEOUS NARRATION (presumably) occurs at the same time as they do ("Jim is now walking down the street; he sees Joan and greets her . . . "); finally, an INTERCALATED NARRATION is temporally situated between two moments of the action recounted and is characteristic of epistolary narratives (*Pamela*) and diary narratives (*Nausea*). **3.** TELLING, in Todorov's terminology: narration is to REPRESENTATION as telling is to SHOWING. **4.** DISCOURSE, in Ricardou's terminology: narration is to FICTION as discourse is to STORY. ¶Genette 1980; Prince 1982; Ricardou 1967; Todorov 1966, 1981.

narrative. The recounting (as product and process, object and act, structure and structuration) of one or more real or fictitious EVENTS communicated by one, two, or several (more or less overt) NARRATORS to one, two, or several (more or less overt) NARRATEES. Such (possibly interesting) texts as "Electrons are constituents of atoms," "Mary is tall and Peter is small," "All men are mortal; Socrates is a man; Socrates is mortal," and "Roses are red / Violets are blue / Sugar is sweet / And so are you" do not constitute narratives, since they do not represent any event. Moreover, a dramatic performance representing (many fascinating) events does not constitute a narrative either, since these events, rather than being recounted, occur directly on stage. On the other hand, even such possibly uninteresting texts as "The man opened the door," "The goldfish died," and "The glass fell on the floor" are narratives, according to this definition. ¶In order to distinguish narrative from mere event description, some narratologists (Labov, Prince, Rimmon-Kenan) have defined it as the recounting of at least two real or fictive events (or one situation and one event), neither of which logically presupposes or entails the other. In order to distinguish it from the recounting of a random series of situations and events, narratologists (Danto, Greimas, Todorov) have also argued that narrative must have a continuant subject and constitute a whole. ¶The narrative media of representation are diverse (oral, written, and sign language, for example, still or moving pictures, gestures, music, or any ordered combination thereof). So are the forms narrative can take (in the domain of verbal narrative alone, we find novels and romances, novellas and short stories, history, biography and autobiography, epics, myths, folktales, legends and ballads, news reports, spontaneous accounts in ordinary conversation, and so on). As for its distribution, narrative appears in every human society known to history and anthropology. Indeed, all (average) human beings know how to produce and process narrative at a very early age. ¶Considered as a structure or product, and following Labov's well-known characterization, narrative can be said to exhibit at least a COMPLICATING ACTION and (when "complete" or "fully developed") as many as six basic macrostructural elements: ABSTRACT, ORIENTATION, complicating action, EVALUATION, RESULT or RESOLUTION, and CODA. More specifically, and following the famous two-tier structuralist model, narrative can be said to have two parts: STORY and DISCOURSE. ¶The story always involves temporal sequence (it consists of at least one modification of a state of affairs obtaining at time t_0 into another state of affairs obtaining at time t_n), and this is its most distinctive feature. Of course, temporal relations between the situations and events making up a story are not the only ones possible: these situations and events may be related causally, for example. Moreover, in a "true" narrative as opposed to the mere recounting of a random series of changes of state, these situations and events also make up a whole, a SEQUENCE the first and last major terms of which are partial repetitions of each other, a structure having—to use Aristotle's terminology—a BEGINNING, a MIDDLE, and an END. ¶If the Aristotelian account of story structure has been exceedingly influential, the most seminal account of that structure in modern NARRATOLOGY has probably been that of Vladimir Propp, who developed the notion of FUNCTION, argued that every (Russian fairy) tale consists of one or more MOVES, and categorized tale participants in terms of the fundamental ROLES they may assume. ¶Further investigation into the nature of functions and roles have led Greimas and his school to arrive at what is another influential account of story structure, according to which canonical narrative is the representation of a series of events oriented in terms of a goal (equivalent to a JUNCTION between SUBJECT and OBJECT). Specifically, after a CONTRACT between SENDER and SUBJECT (MANIPULATION) whereby the latter acquires COMPETENCE and undertakes to attain an Object (for the benefit of a RECEIVER), the Subject goes on its QUEST and, as a result of a series of TESTS (PERFORMANCE), fulfills or fails to fulfill the contract and is (justly) rewarded or (unjustly) punished (SANCTION). ¶The "same" given story can be told differently in narratives adopting different discourses, and conversely, different stories can be told in terms of the same discourse (with the same chronological arrangement of events, for instance, the same FOCALIZATION, SPEED, FREQUENCY, and DISTANCE, and the same kind of inscription of narrator and narratee in the narrative text). ¶The very depiction of a narrator recounting situations and events to a narratee emphasizes the fact that narrative is not only a product but also a process, not merely an object but also an act which occurs in a certain situation because of certain factors and with a view of fulfilling certain functions (informing, diverting attention, entertaining, persuading, etc.). More specifically, narrative is a context-bound exchange between two parties, an exchange resulting from the desire of (at least one of) these parties, and the "same" story can have a different worth in different situations (A wants to know what happened, but B does not; A understands an account in one way and B in another). This sheds light on the tendency of many narrative texts to underline the contract between narrator and narratee, that contract on which the very existence of the narrative depends: I will tell you a story if you promise to be good; I will listen to you if you make it valuable; or, more literarily, a tale for a day of survival (*Arabian Nights*), a story for a night of love ("Sarrasine"), a diary for redemption (*Vipers' Tangle*). This also explains why unsolicited narratives, in particular, must awaken and maintain desire in the audience by relying on the dynamics of SURPRISE and SUSPENSE; why narrators try to make it clear that their narrative has a POINT; and why the very shape of a narrative is affected by the situation in which it occurs and the goal which it seeks to attain, with the sender of the message giving certain kinds of information, disposing it in a certain way, adopting one kind of focalization as opposed to another, underscoring the importance or strangeness of certain details, so that the receiver can better process the information in terms of certain imperatives and ends. ¶Of the many functions that narrative can have, there are some that it excels at or is unique in fulfilling. By definition, narrative always recounts one or more events; but, as etymology suggests (the term *narrative* is related to the Latin GNARUS), it also represents a particular mode of knowledge. It does not simply mirror what happens; it explores and devises what can happen. It does not merely recount changes of state; it constitutes and interprets them as signifying parts of signifying wholes (situations, practices, persons, societies). Narrative can thus shed light on individual fate or group destiny, the unity of a self or the nature of a collectivity. Through showing that apparently heterogeneous situations and events can make up one signifying structure (or vice versa) and, more particularly, through providing its own brand of order and coherence to (a possible) reality, it furnishes examples for its transformation or redefinition and effects a mediation between the law of what is and the desire for what may be. Most crucially, perhaps, by marking off distinct moments in time and setting up relations among them, by discovering meaningful designs in temporal series, by establishing an end already partly contained in the beginning and a beginning already partly containing the end, by exhibiting the meaning of time and/or providing it with meaning, narrative deciphers time and indicates how to decipher it. In sum, narrative illuminates temporality and humans as temporal beings. ¶Adam 1984, 1985; Aristotle 1968; Bal 1985; Barthes 1974, 1975; Benjamin 1969; Booth 1983; Bremond 1973, 1980; Brooks 1984; Chafe 1980; Chambers 1984; Chatman 1978; Courtés 1976; Culler 1981; Danto 1965; Van Dijk 1976a, 1976b; Doležel 1973, 1976; Freytag 1894; Genette 1980, 1983; Genot 1979, 1984; Greimas 1970, 1983a, 1983b; Grimes 1975; Hénault 1983; Janik 1973; Johnson and Mandler 1980; Kermode 1967; Kloepfer 1980; Labov 1972; Larivaille 1974; Lemon and Reis 1965; Matejka and Pomorska 1971; Martin 1986; Mink 1969–70, 1978; Mitchell 1981; Pavel 1985; Prince 1982; Propp 1968; Ricoeur 1984, 1985; Rimmon-Kenan 1983; Sacks 1972; Scholes and Kellogg 1966; Segre 1979; Smith 1981; Stanzel 1984; Stein 1982; Todorov 1966, 1978, 1981; White 1973. See also CAUSALITY, DOUBLE LOGIC OF NARRATIVE, FREYTAG'S PYRAMID, NARRATION, NARRATIVITY, ORDER, PLOT, POST HOC ERGO PROPTER HOC FALLACY.

narrative clause. A clause the displacement of which across a TEMPORAL JUNCTURE leads to a change in the semantic interpretation of the original narrative sequence. In "John went to greet the couple. The man stopped talking, and the woman started to smile. John decided they were nice," both "John went to greet the couple" and "John decided they were nice" are narrative clauses. ¶Narrative clauses constitute the skeleton of the narrative, and as opposed to FREE CLAUSES and RESTRICTED CLAUSES, they are locked in a certain position in the narrative sequence. ¶Labov 1972; Labov and Waletzky 1967. See also COORDINATE CLAUSES, DISPLACEMENT SET.

narrative closure. A conclusion giving the feeling that a narrative or narrative SEQUENCE has come to an END and providing it with an ultimate unity and coherence, an end creating in the receiver a feeling of appropriate completion and finality. ¶Hamon 1975; Kermode 1967; Miller 1981; Smith 1968; Torgovnick 1981. See also CODA.

narrative code. The system of norms, rules, and constraints in terms of which a narrative MESSAGE signifies. This system is not monolithic: it conjoins, combines, and orders a set of CODES or subcodes (the HERMENEUTIC CODE, the PROAIRETIC CODE, the SYMBOLIC CODE, etc.). ¶Barthes 1974, 1981a; Prince 1977, 1982.

narrative competence. The ability to produce and understand narratives. One of the goals of NARRATOLOGY is to characterize narrative competence. ¶Hamon 1981; Prince 1981–82. See also LANGUE.

narrative contract. The agreement between the NARRATOR and the NARRATEE, the teller and his or her audience, underlying the very existence of a NARRATIVE and affecting its very shape: an act of narration supplies something which is (to be) exchanged for something else (I will tell you a story if you promise to be good; I will listen to you if you make it valuable; or, more literarily, a tale for a day of survival as in *Arabian Nights,* a story for a night of love as in "Sarrasine," a diary for redemption as in *Vipers' Tangle*). ¶Barthes 1974; Brooks 1984; Chambers 1984.

narrative domain. The set of MOVES pertaining (mainly) to a given character (and his or her allies). From a semantic point of view, a narrative domain is governed by a number of maxims or rules establishing what is or could be the case, regulating the character's knowledge, setting his or her priorities, and, most generally, guiding him or her in assessing a situation and reacting to it. ¶A narrative in which all the narrative domains are governed by identical sets of maxims and rules is said to be semantically homogeneous. When the sets are not identical, the narrative is semantically heterogeneous or partitioned. Should only certain classes of maxims and rules—say, ontological and epistemological ones—be in force in all the narrative domains, the narrative would be said to be ontologically and epistemologically homogeneous. In other words, a narrative could be ontologically homogeneous but axiologically partitioned, or epistemologically homogeneous but axiologically partitioned, and so on. ¶Pavel 1980, 1985. See also MODALITY.

narrative grammar. A series of statements and formulas interrelated by an ordered set of rules and accounting for (structural aspects of) a particular set of narratives or the set of all and only possible narratives. ¶Among the various narrative grammars that have been developed, the STORY GRAMMARS devised by students of cognitive psychology and artificial intelligence have been very influential: they attempt to specify the basic constituents of the NARRATED and to describe their interrelations, and they help to investigate the effects of structure and content variables on memory and the comprehension of texts. ¶Narrative grammars developed along structuralist and text-linguistic lines and trying to specify the syntax and semantics of plot (Pavel), the macrostructural elements of narrative and their articulation (van Dijk), or the constituents of both story and discourse and their interrelations have also been proposed. Such grammars (often) aim at completeness (accounting for all and only narratives), explicitness (indicating, with a minimum of interpretation left to their users, how a narrative can be produced and/or understood by utilizing a specific set of rules), and empirical plausibility (being in line with what is known about cognitive and social determinants). ¶A grammar of narrative might ultimately consist of the following interconnected parts: (1) a finite number of (REWRITE) RULES generating the MACRO- and MICRO-STRUCTURES of all and only sequences of narrated situations and events; (2) a semantic component interpreting these structures (characterizing both the global macrostructural and the local microstructural content); (3) a finite set of (TRANS-FORMATIONAL) RULES operating on the interpreted structures and accounting for

narrative discourse (FREQUENCY, RHYTHM, SPEED, narratorial intrusions, etc.); (4) a pragmatic component (specifying the cognitive and communicative factors which affect the processing, TELLABILITY, and suitability of the output of the first three parts of the grammar); and (5) an expression component, allowing for the translation of the information provided by the other components into a given medium of representation (for example, written English). ¶Black and Bower 1980; Bruce 1978; Bruce and Newman 1978; Chabrol 1973; Colby 1973; van Dijk 1972, 1976a, 1980; Füger 1972; Genot 1979, 1984; Glenn 1978; Georges 1970; Hendricks 1973; Kintsch and van Dijk 1975; Lakoff 1972; Mandler and Johnson 1977; Pavel 1976, 1985; Prince 1973, 1980, 1982; Rumelhart 1975; Ryan 1979; Schank 1975; Thorndyke 1975; Todorov 1969; Wilensky 1978. See also METALANGUAGE.

narrative level. See DIEGETIC LEVEL.

narrative medium. The SUBSTANCE of the EXPRESSION plane of narrative; the medium in terms of which the narrative manifests itself. With written narrative, for example, that medium is written language; with oral narrative, it is oral language. ¶Chatman 1978. See also MANIFESTATION.

narrative program. A SYNTAGM at the level of narrative SURFACE STRUCTURE representing a change of state effected by an ACTOR and affecting another (or the same) actor. Narrative programs can be simple (when they do not require the realization of another narrative program for their own realization) or complex (when they do). ¶Greimas 1970, 1983a; Greimas and

Courtés 1982; Hénault 1983. See also ACT, NARRATIVE TRAJECTORY.

narrative proposition. See PROPOSITION.

narrative report. A narrator's account, in his or her own words, of a character's utterances or thoughts. ¶Chatman 1978.

narrative schema. A general FRAME in terms of which NARRATIVE is organized. ¶According to the canonical narrative schema, after a given order of things is disturbed, a CONTRACT is established between the SENDER and the SUBJECT to bring about a new order or reinstate the old one (MANIPULATION). The Subject, who has been qualified through the contract along the axes of desire, obligation, knowledge, and/or ability (COMPETENCE), goes through a number of TESTS to fulfill its part of the contract (PERFORMANCE) and is rewarded (or punished) by the Sender (SANCTION). ¶Greimas 1970, 1983a; Greimas and Courtés 1982; Hénault 1983; Larivaille 1974.

narrative sentence. A sentence that refers to at least two temporally distinct situations or events but describes (is about) only the earliest one. "Emperor Napoleon was born in 1769" constitutes a narrative sentence: it refers both to an event occurring in 1769 and to a situation obtaining between 1804 and 1815 (when Napoleon was emperor) but it describes only the former. Narrative sentences are important signs of the teleological determination of narrative. ¶Danto 1965. See also END.

narrative situation. The mediating process through which the NARRATED is presented. Stanzel characterized the kinds and degrees of "mediacy" found in narrative by using the categories of PERSON, MODE, and PERSPECTIVE. (Is there a HETERODIEGETIC or a HOMODIEGETIC NARRATOR? Are the narrated situations and events presented panoramically—say, in terms of an OVERT NARRATOR—or scenically, in terms of a character-REFLECTOR? Is the POINT OF VIEW located in the story's PROTAGONIST or its center of action, or is it located outside the story or its center of action?) He isolated three fundamental narrative situations: AUTHORIAL (AUKTORIALE ERZÄHLSITUATION), in which external perspective dominates; FIGURAL or PERSONAL (PERSONALE ERZÄHLSITUATION), in which a reflector mode dominates; and FIRST-PERSON (ICH ERZÄHLSITUATION), in which a homodiegetic narrator dominates. ¶In a more recent discussion in which Genette defines narrative situation according to person (homodiegetic or heterodiegetic narrator), FOCALIZATION (zero, external, or internal), and NARRATIVE LEVEL (EXTRADIEGETIC or INTRADIEGETIC), Genette characterizes twelve different narrative situations. He also underlines the fact that if such categories as DISTANCE or temporal relation of NARRATION and narrated were taken into account, many more narrative situations could be characterized. ¶Cohn 1981; Genette 1983; Lintvelt 1981; Stanzel 1964, 1971, 1984. See also FOCUS OF NARRATION.

narrative statement. An elementary constituent of DISCOURSE independent of the particular medium of narrative MANIFESTATION: the discourse can be said to state the story through a connected set of narrative statements. ¶There are two basic kinds of narrative statement: PROCESS STATE-

MENTS (in the mode of *Do* or *Happen*) and STASIS STATEMENTS (in the mode of IS). ¶Chatman 1978. See also ACT, EVENT, HAPPENING, STATE.

narrative strategy. In recounting a narrative, the set of narrative procedures followed or narrative devices used to achieve some specific goal. ¶Souvage 1965.

narrative trajectory. A set of logically connected NARRATIVE PROGRAMS. A narrative trajectory involves the same ACTANT, and each one of its constituent narrative programs corresponds to an ACTANTIAL ROLE. In its canonical narrative trajectory, for example, the SUBJECT is established as such by the SENDER, qualified (made competent) along the axes of desire, ability, knowledge, and obligation, realized as a performing Subject, recognized as one, and rewarded ¶Greimas and Courtés 1982.

narrative world. The set or collection of MO-TIFS in a given narrative (or part thereof) that are authenticated and thus given the status of facts. ¶A distinction can be made between an actual (or absolute) narrative world and a possible (or relative) one: the former constitutes the sphere of "reality" for the individuals in a narrative; the latter would result from world-creating and/or world-representing acts by these individuals, such as forming beliefs, wishing, dreaming, predicting, or imagining (Ryan). ¶Doležel 1976; Ryan 1985. See also AU-THENTICATION FUNCTION.

narrativics. NARRATOLOGY. ¶The term, introduced by Ihwe, has not gained much currency. Some students of narrative at times make a distinction between narrativ-ics and narratology: the former develops models or grammars accounting for (the structure of) narrative; the latter uses these models or grammars to study particular narratives. ¶Genot 1979; Ihwe 1972. See also NARRATIVE GRAMMAR.

narrativity. The set of properties characterizing NARRATIVE and distinguishing it from nonnarrative; the formal and contextual features making a narrative more or less narrative, as it were. ¶The degree of narrativity of a given narrative depends partly on the extent to which that narrative fulfills a receiver's desire by representing oriented temporal wholes (prospectively from BEGIN-NING to END and retrospectively from end to beginning), involving a CONFLICT, consisting of discrete, specific, and positive situations and events, and meaningful in terms of a human(ized) project and world. ¶Brooks 1984; Genot 1979; Greimas 1970; Kloepfer 1980; Prince 1982. See also DOU-BLE LOGIC OF NARRATIVE, MIDDLE, POST HOC ERGO PROPTER HOC FALLACY.

narratized discourse. A TYPE OF DISCOURSE whereby a character's utterances or verbal thoughts are represented, in words that are the narrator's, as acts among other acts; a discourse about words uttered (or thoughts) equivalent to a discourse not about words. For example, should a given character have said at one point, "Well! that's settled then! I'll meet you at the station!," narratized discourse might render it as "She made an appointment to meet her." ¶Along with REPORTED DISCOURSE (DIRECT DISCOURSE) and TRANSPOSED DIS-COURSE (INDIRECT DISCOURSE), narratized (or narrated or narrativized) discourse is, in

Genette's view, one of the three basic ways of representing characters' utterances and verbal thoughts. ¶Genette 1980, 1983.

narratized speech. NARRATIZED DISCOURSE, especially narratized discourse whereby a character's utterances (as opposed to thoughts) are represented. ¶Genette 1980, 1983.

narratology. **1.** The (structuralist-inspired) theory of NARRATIVE. Narratology studies the nature, form, and functioning of narrative (regardless of medium of representation) and tries to characterize NARRATIVE COMPETENCE. More particularly, it examines what all and only narratives have in common (at the level of STORY, NARRATING, and their relations) as well as what enables them to be different from one another, and it attempts to account for the ability to produce and understand them. ¶The term was proposed by Todorov. **2.** The study of narrative as a verbal mode of representation of temporally ordered situations and events (Genette). In this restricted sense, narratology disregards the level of story in itself (it does not attempt to formulate a grammar of stories or plots, for instance) and focuses on the possible relations between story and narrative text, NARRATING and narrative text, and story and narrating. Specifically, it investigates problems of TENSE, MOOD, and VOICE. **3.** The study of given (sets of) narratives in terms of models elaborated by so-called NARRATIVICS (Genot). This acceptation of the term is rare. ¶Bal 1977, 1985; Genette 1983; Genot 1979; Mathieu-Colas 1986; Pavel 1985; Prince 1981–82, 1982; Todorov 1969. See also LANGUE, NARRATIVE GRAMMAR, PAROLE.

narrator. The one who narrates, as inscribed in the text. There is at least one narrator per narrative, located at the same DIEGETIC LEVEL as the NARRATEE he or she is addressing. In a given narrative, there may, of course, be several different narrators, each addressing in turn a different narratee or the same one. ¶A narrator may be more or less overt, knowledgeable, ubiquitous, self-conscious, and reliable, and s/he may be situated at a greater or lesser DISTANCE from the situations and events narrated, the characters, and/or the narratee. This distance can be temporal (I narrate events that occurred three hours or three years ago), discursive (I narrate in my own words what a character said, or I use his or her own words), intellectual (I am intellectually superior to my narratee, or equal or inferior to him or her), moral (I am more or less virtuous than the characters), and so on. ¶Whether or not s/he is overt, knowledgeable, self-conscious, or reliable, the narrator may be EXTRADIEGETIC, or INTRADIEGETIC. Furthermore, the narrator may be heterodiegetic or homodiegetic and, in the latter case, function as a PROTAGONIST in the events recounted *(Great Expectations, Jouney to the End of the Night, Kiss Me Deadly),* an important character *(All the King's Men, The Great Gatsby),* a minor one *(A Study in Scarlet),* or even a mere observer ("A Rose for Emily"). ¶The narrator, who is immanent to the narrative, must be distinguished from the real or concrete AUTHOR, who is not: *Nausea,* "Intimacy," "The Wall," and "Erostratus" have the same author—

65

Sartre—but different narrators. ¶The narrator must also be distinguished from the IMPLIED AUTHOR: the latter does not recount situations and events (but is taken to be accountable for their selection, distribution, and combination); moreover, s/he is inferred from the entire text rather than inscribed in it as a teller. Though the distinction can be problematic (for example, in the case of an ABSENT or maximally COVERT NARRATOR: "Hills Like White Elephants"), it is sometimes very clear (for example, in the cases of such HOMODIEGETIC NARRATIVES as *Great Expectations* or "Haircut"). ¶Bal 1981a; Booth 1983; Chatman 1978; Ducrot and Todorov 1979; Friedemann 1910; Genette 1980, 1983; Kayser 1958; Prince 1982; Scholes and Kellogg 1966; Suleiman 1980; Tacca 1973. See also GNARUS, HETERODIEGETIC NARRATOR, HOMODIEGETIC NARRATOR, OVERT NARRATOR, PERSON, RELIABLE NARRATOR, SELF-CONSCIOUS NARRATOR, VOICE.

narrator-agent. A NARRATOR who is a character in the situations and events recounted and has some measurable effect in them: Gil Blas, in the novel by the same name, is a narrator-agent. ¶Ducrot and Todorov 1979. See also HOMODIEGETIC NARRATOR, NARRATOR-WITNESS.

narrator-I. The "I" of a HOMODIEGETIC NARRATOR in his or her role as NARRATOR and not as CHARACTER. In "I drank a glass of beer," the "I" who tells about the drinking is the narrator-I, whereas the "I" who drank is the CHARACTER-I. ¶Prince 1982. See also FIRST-PERSON NARRATIVE.

narrator-witness. In a HOMODIEGETIC NARRATIVE, a NARRATOR of whom practically nothing is known beyond the fact of his or her existence *(The Brothers Karamazov).* ¶Ducrot and Todorov 1979. See also NARRATOR-AGENT.

narreme. In Dorfman's terminology, a CARDINAL FUNCTION, a KERNEL, a NUCLEUS. ¶Dorfman 1969; Wittmann 1975.

naturalization. The network of devices through which the receiver of a narrative relates it to an already known model of reality and thus reduces its strangeness. ¶Whereas MOTIVATION is author-oriented, naturalization is reader- or receiver-oriented. ¶Chatman 1978; Culler 1975; Rimmon-Kenan 1983. See also VERISIMILITUDE.

natural narrative. A narrative occurring spontaneously in "normal," everyday conversation. The term is supposed to distinguish narratives produced without deliberation ("naturally") from narratives that have a "constructed" character and appear in specific story-telling contexts. ¶Van Dijk 1974–75; Pratt 1977.

nesting. See EMBEDDING. ¶Barthes 1974.

neutral narrative type. A type of narrative characterized by EXTERNAL FOCALIZATION. Along with the AUCTORIAL and ACTORIAL NARRATIVE TYPES, the neutral narrative type ("The Killers") is one of three basic classes in Lintvelt's typology. ¶Genette 1983; Lintvelt 1981. See also BEHAVIORIST NARRATIVE, DRAMATIC MODE, POINT OF VIEW.

neutral omniscience. One of eight possible POINTS OF VIEW according to Friedman's classification: neutral omniscience characterizes the heterodiegetic and omniscient but nonintrusive, IMPERSONAL NARRATOR *(Lord of the Flies).* ¶N. Friedman 1955b.

See also EDITORIAL OMNISCIENCE.

nonfocalization. See ZERO FOCALIZATION.

nonfocalized narrative. A narrative having ZERO FOCALIZATION *(Vanity Fair, Adam Bede)*. ¶Bal 1977, 1981a; Genette 1980, 1983; Rimmon-Kenan 1983; Vitoux 1982.

nonnarrated narrative. A narrative with an ABSENT NARRATOR; a narrative presenting situations and events with a minimum amount of narratorial mediation ("Hills Like White Elephants"). ¶Chatman 1978. See also MIMESIS, SHOWING.

nucleus. A BOUND MOTIF; a CARDINAL FUNCTION; a KERNEL *(noyau)*. As opposed to CATALYSES, nuclei are logically essential to the narrative action and cannot be eliminated without destroying its causal-chronological coherence. ¶Barthes 1975; Chatman 1978.

O

object. An ACTANT or fundamental ROLE at the level of deep narrative structure, in the Greimassian model. The Object (analogous to Propp's SOUGHT-FOR PERSON and Souriau's SUN) is looked for by the SUBJECT. ¶Greimas 1970, 1983a, 1983b; Greimas and Courtés 1982; Hénault 1983. See also ACTANTIAL MODEL.

objective narrative. **1.** A narrative characterized by the narrator's attitude of detachment toward the situations and events recounted. **2.** A BEHAVIORIST NARRATIVE. ¶Brooks and Warren 1959; Hough 1970; Magny 1972; Romberg 1962; van

Rossum-Guyon 1970. See also DRAMATIC MODE, SUBJECTIVE NARRATIVE.

omnipresent narrator. A ubiquitous narrator; a narrator with the capacity to be in two or more different spaces at the same time or to move freely back and forth between scenes occurring in different places. ¶Omnipresent narrators are typical of historiography and are not necessarily omniscient. Conversely, OMNISCIENT NARRATORS are not necessarily omnipresent: the narrator of *Mrs. Dalloway* is, at times, omniscient but not omnipresent. ¶Chatman 1978.

omniscient narrator. A narrator who knows (practically) everything about the situations and events recounted *(Tom Jones, The Mill on the Floss, Eugénie Grandet)*. Such a narrator has an OMNISCIENT POINT OF VIEW and tells more than any and all the characters know. ¶Booth 1983; Chatman 1978; N. Friedman 1955b; Genette 1980; Prince 1982; Todorov 1981. See also ANALYTIC AUTHOR, AUTHORIAL NARRATIVE SITUATION, OMNIPRESENT NARRATOR, POINT OF VIEW.

omniscient point of view. The POINT OF VIEW adopted by an OMINISCIENT NARRATOR; VISION from behind. Analogous to ZERO FOCALIZATION, omniscient point of view is characteristic of traditional or classical narrative *(Adam Bede, Tom Jones, Vanity Fair)*. ¶Booth 1983; Chatman 1978; N. Friedman 1955b; Genette 1980; Prince 1982. See also LIMITED POINT OF VIEW.

opponent. **1.** An ACTANT or fundamental ROLE at the level of deep structure, in Greimas's early model of narrative. The Opponent (analogous to Propp's VILLAIN and FALSE HERO and to Souriau's MARS) opposes the SUBJECT. **2.** In Greimas's more recent model of narrative, a negative AUXILIANT that is represented, at the surface level, by an ACTOR different from the one representing the SUBJECT. The Opponent, who comes into conflict with the Subject incidentally and/or represents a momentary obstacle for it, should not be confused with the ANTISUBJECT, who is a quester, like the Subject, and has aims that are at cross purposes with those of the Subject. ¶Greimas 1983a, 1983b; Greimas and Courtés 1982; Hénault 1983. See also ACTANTIAL MODEL, ANTIDONOR.

order. The set of relations between the order in which events (are said to) occur and the order in which they are recounted. ¶Events can be recounted in the order of their occurrence: in "Joan ate, then she went out," CHRONOLOGICAL ORDER is observed. On the other hand, there can be discordances between the two orders, as in "Joan went out after she ate"; ANACHRONIES (RETROSPECTIONS or ANTICIPATIONS, ANALEPSES or PROLEPSES, FLASHBACKS or FLASHFORWARDS) then obtain. In some cases an event may be deprived of any temporal connection with other events (it may be dateless): the result is an ACHRONY. In other cases, the unfolding of events may obey a nonchronological principle rather than a chronological one: the result is a SYLLEPSIS. ¶Chatman 1978; Genette 1980; Prince 1982. See also FABULA, PLOT, SJUŽET, STORY.

orientation. In Labov's terminology, the part of a NARRATIVE which identifies the (initial) spatiotemporal situation in which the events recounted took place. If a narrative is taken to constitute a series of answers to certain questions, the orientation is that constituent of it answering the questions "Who?" "When?" "What?" and "Where?" ¶Labov 1972; Pratt 1977.

ostraneniye. See DEFAMILIARIZATION.

overt narrator. A NARRATOR presenting situations and events with more than a minimum of narratorial mediation; an INTRUSIVE NARRATOR *(Eugénie Grandet, Barchester Towers, Tom Jones, Tristram Shandy).* ¶Chatman 1978. See also COVERT NARRATOR, DRAMATIZED NARRATOR, MEDIATED NARRATION.

pace. The regulating of SPEED; the proportioning of TEMPOS in a narrative. ¶Brooks and Warren 1959. See also DURATION, RHYTHM.

panorama. The rendering of situations and events from a distance, in nonscenic terms (as opposed to DRAMA); SUMMARY. ¶Lubbock 1965; Souvage 1965. See also PICTORIAL TREATMENT, PICTURE, SCALE, SCENE.

paradigm. A class of elements all of which can occupy the same position in a given context. Two units *u* and *u'* (say, *man* and *boy*) belong to the same paradigm if there exist two syntagmatic chains *tuv* and *tu'v* (consider *The man ate* and *The boy ate*). ¶Ducrot and Todorov 1979; Greimas and Courtés 1982; Saussure 1966. See also SYNTAGM.

paralepsis. An ALTERATION that consists in giving more information (not less, as in

PARALIPSIS) than should presumably be given in terms of the FOCALIZATION code governing a narrative. Should EXTERNAL FOCALIZATION be adopted, for instance, and should the thoughts of a character suddenly be reported, a paralepsis is said to obtain. ¶Genette 1980.

paralipsis. An ALTERATION that consists in giving less information (not more, as in PARALEPSIS) than should presumably be given in terms of the FOCALIZATION code governing a narrative; a lateral ELLIPSIS whereby it is not an intervening event that goes unmentioned but rather one or more components in the situation that is being recounted. In *The Murder of Roger Ackroyd,* for example, the FOCALIZER is also the murderer, yet until the end, this fact—which he knows perfectly well—is omitted from his thoughts and thus concealed from the reader. ¶Genette 1980.

parole. The individual utterance or speech act (as opposed to the LANGUE or language system which it manifests and which makes it possible). ¶The Saussurean opposition between *langue* (which constitutes the proper object of linguistics) and *parole* is analogous to that between CODE and MESSAGE, SCHEMA and use, or competence and performance. It has had a profound influence on the study of signifying systems and, more particularly, on NARRATOLOGY: the latter can be said to study the *langue* of narrative, the system of rules and norms accounting for the production and understanding of individual narratives (equivalent to *parole*). ¶Greimas and Courtés 1982; Saussure 1966.

participant. An ACTOR; an EXISTENT involved in the situations and events recounted and

having some effect on them (as opposed to a PROP). ¶Grimes 1975.

patient. Along with the AGENT, one of two fundamental ROLES in Bremond's typology. Whereas patients are affected by certain processes (and, more specifically, may constitute victims or beneficiaries), agents initiate these processes and influence the patients, modify their situation (improving or worsening it), or maintain it (for the good or the bad). ¶Bremond 1973; Scholes 1974.

pattern. A significant arrangement of repetitions (in the narrated situations and events). E. M. Forster characterized a number of PLOT patterns, such as the "hour-glass" *(Thaïs, The Ambassadors)* or the "grand chain" *(Roman Pictures).* ¶Brooks and Warren 1959; Forster 1927; Frye 1957; Souvage 1965.

pause. A canonical narrative TEMPO; along with ELLIPSIS, SCENE, SUMMARY, and STRETCH, one of the fundamental narrative SPEEDS. When some part of the narrative text or some DISCOURSE TIME corresponds to no elapsing of STORY TIME, pause obtains (and the narrative can be said to come to a stop). ¶A pause can be occasioned by a description or by a narrator's commentarial excursuses. ¶Chatman 1978; Genette 1980; Prince 1982. See also COMMENTARY, DESCRIPTIVE PAUSE, DURATION.

perceptual point of view. The physical perception through which a situation or event is apprehended. ¶Chatman 1978. See also CONCEPTUAL POINT OF VIEW, POINT OF VIEW.

performance. In Greimassian terminology, the NARRATIVE PROGRAM of a SUBJECT that has acquired COMPETENCE. Performance consists in the transformation of a given state of affairs and, more specifically, culminates in the CONJUNCTION of Subject and OBJECT. ¶Adam 1984, 1985; Greimas 1983a, 1983b; Greimas and Courtés 1976, 1982. See also DECISIVE TEST, NARRATIVE SCHEMA.

performative. An utterance that is used to do rather than to say something, to perform an act by means of language rather than to state that something is or is not the case: "I promise to come at five" and "I bet you a dollar that it will rain tomorrow" are performatives, and by uttering them, the speaker actually makes a promise or a bet. More specifically, they are explicit performatives (performing the very illocutionary act to which they refer) as opposed to such implicit or primary performatives as "I'll be there at five" and "A dollar," which do not contain a verb or expression naming the act but can be used to make a promise or a bet. ¶The theory of SPEECH ACTS originates in Austin's distinction between performatives and CONSTATIVES (utterances like "Napoleon won the battle of Austerlitz" that report events or states of affairs in certain worlds and consequently are "either true or false" in these worlds). However, as Austin goes on to argue, constatives themselves are performatives, since saying (asserting, stating, reporting) that something is or is not the case constitutes a kind of doing. Indeed, any utterance or set of utterances can be viewed as performative. ¶If narrative can be said to "constate," to report that certain situations and events are the case in certain worlds, it can also be said to perform (at the very least) the act of reporting.

¶Austin 1962; Lyons 1977; Pratt 1977. See also ILLOCUTIONARY ACT.

peripeteia. See PERIPETY.

peripety. The inversion (REVERSAL) from one state of affairs to its opposite. For example, an action seems destined for success but suddenly moves toward failure, or vice versa. ¶According to Aristotle, peripety (PERIPETEIA) is, along with RECOGNITION (ANAGNORISIS), the most potent means of ensuring the tragic effect. ¶Aristotle 1968.

perlocutionary act. An act performed *by means of* saying something and describable in terms of the effect which the ILLOCUTIONARY ACT performed *in* saying that something has on the ADDRESSEE. When I say to someone "I promise to be there," I (may) accomplish, through my promising, the perlocutionary act of convincing him or her of my good faith. Along with a LOCUTIONARY ACT and an illocutionary act, a perlocutionary act is (possibly) involved in the performance of a SPEECH ACT. ¶Little progress has been made in the study of perlocutionary acts, and they have been increasingly absent from explorations in speech act theory. However, when NARRATIVES are viewed as speech acts, they are sometimes said to accomplish certain perlocutionary acts (e.g., convincing, frightening, or entertaining their addressees). ¶Austin 1962; Lyons 1977; Pratt 1977.

person. The set of relations between the NARRATOR (and NARRATEE) and the story narrated. ¶A distinction is commonly made between FIRST-PERSON NARRATIVES (the narrator of which is a character in the situations and events recounted) and THIRD-PERSON NARRATIVES (the narrator of which is not a character in the situations and events recounted). Another category is that of the SECOND-PERSON NARRATIVE (the narratee of which is the main character in the situations and events recounted). ¶Bal 1985; Cohn 1978; Genette 1980, 1983; Prince 1982; Rimmon-Kenan 1983; Stanzel 1984; Tamir 1976. See also VOICE.

persona. In the criticism of narrative fiction, a term that is used to refer to the IMPLIED AUTHOR but that is also commonly used to refer to the NARRATOR. ¶The term was a Latin word designating the actor's mask in classical theater. ¶Booth 1983; Holman 1972; Souvage 1965.

personal narrative situation. See FIGURAL NARRATIVE SITUATION. ¶Stanzel 1964, 1971, 1984.

personale Erzählsituation. See FIGURAL NARRATIVE SITUATION. ¶Stanzel 1964, 1971, 1984.

perspective. FOCALIZATION; POINT OF VIEW. Along with DISTANCE, perspective is one of two main factors regulating narrative information. ¶Genette 1980, 1983; Rimmon 1976.

phatic function. One of the FUNCTIONS OF COMMUNICATION in terms of which any communicative (verbal) act may be structured and oriented. When the communicative act is centered on the CONTACT (rather than one of the other CONSTITUTIVE FACTORS OF COMMUNICATION), it (mainly) has a phatic function. More specifically, those passages in narrative focusing on the psychophysiological connection between narrator and narratee ("Reader, are you still following me, or are you overwhelmed by the details I'm providing?") can be said to fulfill a

phatic function. ¶Jakobson 1960; Malinowski 1953; Prince 1982.

pictorial treatment. In Jamesian terminology and as opposed to DRAMATIC TREATMENT, a nonscenic presentation of some character's view of situations and events; PICTURE. ¶H. James 1972; Lubbock 1965.

picture. A nonscenic rendering of some character's consciousness of a situation. In *The Ambassadors,* Strether's first view of Chad at the play constitutes a picture. ¶In Jamesian terminology, picture is contrasted with DRAMA (which renders scenically the characters' speech and behavior). ¶H. James 1972; Lubbock 1965.

plan. A global semantic framework representing various aspects of reality pertinent to a planner or being advancing toward a GOAL. Narrative frequently consists of sets of interacting plans. ¶Plans are often taken to be equivalent to FRAMES, SCHEMATA, and SCRIPTS, but certain suggestive distinctions have been proposed: a serially ordered, temporally bound frame is a schema; a goal-directed schema is a plan; and a stereotypical plan is a script. ¶Bartlett 1932; Beaugrande 1980; Bruce and Newman 1976.

plot. **1.** The main incidents of a NARRATIVE; the outline of situations and events (thought of as distinct from the CHARACTERS involved in them or the THEMES illustrated by them). ¶These incidents can constitute a structure the main parts of which are characterizable in terms of FREYTAG'S PYRAMID. **2.** The arrangement of incidents; MYTHOS; SJUŽET; the situations and events as presented to the receiver.

¶The Russian Formalists made an influential distinction between *sjužet* and FABULA (or basic STORY material). **3.** The global dynamic (goal-oriented and forward-moving) organization of narrative constituents which is responsible for the thematic interest (indeed, the very intelligibility) of a narrative and for its emotional effect. **4.** A narrative of events with an emphasis on causality, as opposed to story, which is a narrative of events with an emphasis on chronology (Forster). "The king died, and then the queen died" is a story, whereas "The king died, and then the queen died of grief" is a plot. ¶Aristotle 1968; Brooks 1984; Brooks and Warren 1959; Chatman 1978; Crane 1952; Egan 1978; Forster 1927; N. Friedman 1955a, 1975; Frye 1957; Martin 1986; O'Grady 1965; Pavel 1985; Ricoeur 1984; Scholes and Kellogg 1966; Shklovsky 1965b; Tomashevsky 1965. See also DOUBLE PLOT, PLOT TYPOLOGY, SUBPLOT.

plot typology. The systematic determination of PLOT types according to structural or other similarities. For example, plots can be euphoric (fortunate: things change for the better) or dysphoric (fatal: things change for the worse), external (based on outer events and experiences) or internal (based on inner feelings and transactions), simple (lacking PERIPETY and/or RECOGNITION) or complex, epic (episodic, loosely woven) or dramatic (closely knit), and so on. ¶Among the modern attempts to devise a typology of plots, Crane's and Friedman's are particularly noteworthy from the point of view of NARRATOLOGY. Crane offers a tripartite classification: plots of action (involving a change in the protagonist's situation: *The Brothers Karamazov*), plots of character (involving a change in the protagonist's moral character: *The Portrait of a Lady*), and plots of thought (involving a change in the protagonist's thought and feeling: *Marius the Epicurean*). ¶Friedman proposes a more detailed classification, by making further distinctions as to whether the protagonist succeeds or fails, as to whether s/he is responsible and attractive or not, and as to how this complex of factors is supposed to affect the receiver's feelings: **1.** *Plots of Fortune: (a)* the action plot (organized around a problem and a solution and frequent in popular literature: *Treasure Island*); *(b)* the pathetic plot (an attractive but weak protagonist fails, and the unhappy ending inspires pity: *Tess of the D'Urbervilles*); *(c)* the tragic plot (an attractive protagonist is responsible for his or her misfortune, and catharsis is experienced: *Oedipus Rex, King Lear*); *(d)* the punitive plot (an antipathetic though partly admirable protagonist fails: *Richard III, The Treasure of the Sierra Madre*); *(e)* the sentimental plot (an attractive but weak or passive protagonist succeeds in the end: *Bleak House, Anna Christie*); *(f)* the admiration plot (an attractive and responsible protagonist succeeds and arouses respect and admiration: *Tom Sawyer, Mister Roberts*); **2.** *Plots of Character: (a)* the maturing plot (an attractive but naive protagonist acquires maturity: *Portrait of the Artist as a Young Man, Great Expectations, The Portrait of a Lady*); *(b)* the reform plot (an attractive protagonist is responsible for his or her misfortunes but changes for the better: *The Scarlet Letter, The Pillars of the Community*); *(c)* the testing plot (a protagonist fails repeatedly and renounces his or her ideals: *The Sea Gull, Uncle Vanya*); *(d)* the degeneration plot (an attractive protagonist changes for the worse after some important crisis: *The Immoralist*); **3.** *Plots of Thought: (a)* the education plot (the thought of an attractive protagonist improves, but the effect of this improvement on his or her behavior is not shown: *Huckleberry Finn*); *(b)* the revelation plot (the protagonist gets to know his or her own condition: Roald Dahl's "Beware of the Dog"), *(c)* the affective plot (the protagonist changes in attitudes and feelings but not in philosophy: *Pride and Prejudice*); *(d)* the disillusionment plot (the protagonist loses his or her ideals as well as the receiver's sympathy and ends in despair or death: *The Great Gatsby, The Sot-Weed Factor*). ¶Aristotle 1968; Chatman 1968; Crane 1952; Ducrot and Todorov 1979; N. Friedman 1955a, 1975; Pavel 1985; A. Wright 1982.

poetic function. One of the FUNCTIONS OF COMMUNICATION in terms of which any communicative (verbal) act may be structured and oriented. When the communicative act is centered on the MESSAGE for its own sake (rather than on one of the other CONSTITUTIVE FACTORS OF COMMUNICATION), it (mainly) has a poetic function. More specifically, those passages in narrative focusing on the message and underlining its tangibility (drawing attention to its structure, its shape, etc.: "Peter Piper picked a peck of pickled peppers") can be said to fulfill a poetic function. ¶Jakobson 1960; Prince 1982.

point. The *raison d'être* of a NARRATIVE, the reason for which it is recounted and the

essential matter it is getting at (Labov). The point of a narrative is indicated or suggested by a set of evaluative features that show why the situations and events narrated are worth narrating: whereas a pointless narrative might be greeted with a remark like "So what?," a pointed one would be greeted with an acknowledgement of its REPORTABILITY. ¶Labov 1972; Polanyi 1979; Prince 1983. See also ABSTRACT.

point of view. The perceptual or conceptual position in terms of which the narrated situations and events are presented; FOCALIZATION; PERSPECTIVE; VIEWPOINT. The point of view adopted may be that of an OMNISCIENT NARRATOR whose position varies and is sometimes unlocatable and who is (by and large) not subject to perceptual or conceptual restrictions (OMNISCIENT POINT OF VIEW: *Vanity Fair, Adam Bede*). Or else, it may be situated in the diegesis and, more specifically, in a character (INTERNAL POINT OF VIEW: everything is presented strictly in terms of the knowledge, feelings, and perceptions of the same character or different ones). In this case, it may be fixed (the perspective of one and only one character is adopted: *What Maisie Knew*), variable (the perspective of several characters is adopted in turn to present different sequences of events: *The Golden Bowl, The Age of Reason*), or multiple (the same event or sequence of events is narrated more than once, each time in terms of a different perspective: *The Moonstone, The Ring and the Book*). Finally, it may emanate from a focal point situated in the diegesis but outside any of the characters (any thinking or feeling being); it thereby excludes all information on feelings and thoughts and is limited to registering the characters' words and actions, their appearance, and the setting against which they come to the fore (EXTERNAL POINT OF VIEW: "Hills Like White Elephants"). ¶According to this narrow definition (inspired by Genette), point of view ("who sees") should be distinguished from VOICE ("who speaks"): it is not equivalent to expression but institutes the perspective governing expression. Yet, especially since the work of Lubbock on narrative technique, point of view has often been taken to involve not only a perceptual or conceptual apparatus but also factors like the NARRATOR's overtness, the types of treatment favored (DRAMA or PANORAMA), and the TYPES OF DISCOURSE adopted. More generally, it has been taken to spring from the relations between narrator and NARRATING, narrator and NARRATEE, and narrator and NARRATED (Lanser). ¶Several typological descriptions of narrative based on point of view (in the broader rather than narrower sense) have been proposed. Thus, Brooks and Warren (who use the term FOCUS OF NARRATION) offer a quadripartite classification based on two distinctions: between FIRST-PERSON and THIRD-PERSON NARRATIVE and between internal depiction and external observation of events: (1) first person (AUTODIEGETIC NARRATIVE: *Great Expectations*); (2) first-person observer (the narrator is a secondary character in the story recounted: *The Great Gatsby*); (3) author-observer (external point of view: "Hills Like White Elephants"); (4) omniscient author *(Tess of the D'Urbervilles)*.

¶Grimes, who speaks of viewpoint, also distinguishes four basic categories: (1) omniscient viewpoint (equivalent to Brooks and Warren's omniscient author); (2) first-person participant viewpoint (HOMODIEGETIC NARRATIVE with internal point of view); (3) third-person subjective viewpoint (HETERODIEGETIC NARRATIVE with internal point of view); (4) third-person objective viewpoint (external point of view). ¶Pouillon, who prefers to speak of VISION (followed by Todorov, who spoke of ASPECT), has a three-term classification: (1) vision from behind (similar to ZERO FOCALIZATION or omniscient point of view; the narrator tells more than any and all of the characters know: *Tess of the D'Urbervilles*); (2) vision with (similar to internal point of view; the narrator tells only what one or several characters know: *The Ambassadors, The Age of Reason*); (3) vision from without (similar to external point of view; the narrator tells less about certain situations than one or several characters know: "The Killers"). ¶Friedman proposes an eight-term classification, in order of narratorial prominence: (1) EDITORIAL OMNISCIENCE (heterodiegetic, omniscient, and INTRUSIVE NARRATOR: *Tess of the D'Urbervilles, War and Peace*); (1) NEUTRAL OMNISCIENCE (heterodiegetic and omniscient but nonintrusive, IMPERSONAL NARRATOR: *Point Counterpoint, Lord of the Flies*); (3) "I" AS WITNESS (the narrator is a secondary character in the situations and events presented, and the latter are viewed from the periphery rather than from the center: *The Good Soldier, The Great Gatsby*); (4) "I" AS PROTAGONIST (the narrator is the protagonist in the action recounted, and the latter is viewed from the center: *Great Expectations, Huckleberry Finn, The Catcher in the Rye*); (5) MULTIPLE SELECTIVE OMNISCIENCE (HETERODIEGETIC NARRATOR with variable internal point of view: *The Age of Reason, To the Lighthouse*); (6) SELECTIVE OMNISCIENCE (heterodiegetic narrator with fixed internal point of view: *The Ambassadors, A Portrait of the Artist as a Young Man*); (7) the DRAMATIC MODE (heterodiegetic narrator with external point of view: *The Awkward Age*); (8) the CAMERA (the situations and events narrated presumably "just happen" before a neutral recorder and are transmitted by it without ostensible organization or selection: *Goodbye to Berlin*). ¶Stanzel distinguishes between three main types of NARRATIVE SITUATIONS: the AUKTORIALE ERZÄHLSITUATION (characterized by an omniscient narrator: *Tess of the D'Urbervilles, Tom Jones*); the PERSONALE ERZÄHLSITUATION (heterodiegetic narrator with internal point of view: *The Ambassadors*); and the ICH ERZÄHLSITUATION (first-person narrative: *Great Expectations, Nausea*). To these three categories (or ones that are essentially similar), Romberg adds that of the narrator as behaviorist observer ("Hills Like White Elephants"). ¶Uspenskij considers that point of view manifests itself on four different planes—ideological, phraseological, spatiotemporal (narrator's spatial perspective on and temporal distance from narrated), and psychological (narrator's psychological distance from or affinity with narrated)—and he makes a fundamental distinction on each plane between what he calls internal and external point of view (is the perceptual or conceptual position inside or outside the diegesis? does the information conveyed result from an inner view or an outer one?). ¶Doležel arrives at a six-term categorization based on a distinction between the ICH-FORM and the ER-FORM (first-person and third-person narrative) and on a further distinction between three narrative modes: objective (the narrator views the situations and events from the periphery rather than from the center and does not evaluate or comment on them), rhetorical (the narrator views the situations and events from the periphery but is intrusive), and subjective (situations and events are viewed from the center). ¶Finally, Lintvelt proposes a five-term classification: (1) heterodiegetic AUCTORIAL NARRATIVE TYPE (the point of view is that of the heterodiegetic narrator: *Tess of the D'Urbervilles, Tom Jones*); (2) heterodiegetic ACTORIAL NARRATIVE TYPE (the narrator is heterodiegetic but the point of view is that of a character: *The Ambassadors*); (3) heterodiegetic NEUTRAL NARRATIVE TYPE (similar to Friedman's dramatic mode: "The Killers," *Moderato Cantabile*); (4) homodiegetic auctorial narrative type (the point of view is that of the homodiegetic narrator as narrator: *Moby Dick*); (5) homodiegetic actorial narrative type (the point of view is that of the homodiegetic narrator as character: *The Hunger*). ¶Bal 1977, 1983, 1985; Brooks and Warren 1959; Chatman 1978; Cohn 1981; Doležel 1973; N. Friedman 1955b; Füger 1972; Genette 1980, 1983; Grimes 1975; H. James

1972; Lanser 1981; Leibfried 1972; Lintvelt 1981; Lubbock 1965; Pouillon 1946; Prince 1982; Rimmon-Kenan 1983; Romberg 1962; van Rossum-Guyon 1970; Schmid 1973; Stanzel 1964, 1971, 1984; Todorov 1981; Uspenskij 1973; Weimann 1973.

point-of-view character. See FOCALIZER.

point-of-view narrative. A narrative with INTERNAL POINT OF VIEW. ¶Pascal 1977.

polyphonic narrative. See DIALOGIC NARRATIVE. ¶Bakhtin 1981, 1984.

posterior narration. A NARRATION following in time the narrated situations and events, a SUBSEQUENT NARRATING. Posterior narration is characteristic of "classical" or "traditional" narrative. ¶Prince 1982.

post hoc ergo propter hoc fallacy. A confusion, denounced by scholasticism, between consecutiveness and consequence. According to Barthes (following Aristotle), the mainspring of NARRATIVITY is related to an exploitation of this confusion, what-comes-after-X in a narrative being processed as what-is-caused-by-X: given "It started to rain, and Mary became nostalgic," for example, Mary's nostalgia tends to be understood as caused by the weather conditions. ¶Aristotle 1968; Barthes 1975. See also CAUSALITY.

postulated reader. See IMPLIED READER. ¶Booth 1983.

pratton. An AGENT. For Aristotle, the agent, or *pratton,* can be endowed with ETHOS (CHARACTER, the type traits characterizing it) and DIANOIA (THOUGHT). ¶Aristotle 1968. See also CHARACTERIZATION.

praxis. A real ACTION. For Aristotle, MYTHOS (PLOT) consists in the selection and possi-

ble rearrangement of the units constituting LOGOS (the imitation of *praxis*). ¶Aristotle 1968; Chatman 1978.

predicate. In a PREPOSITION or statement, that which asserts something about the subject of the proposition or statement. ¶There are static predicates ("Mary *was sad*") and dynamic ones ("Mary *ate a loaf of bread*"). Furthermore, there are base predicates ("Mary *walked three miles every day*") and transformed predicates (resulting from the simple or complex TRANSFORMATION of a given predicate: "Jane *thought that Mary walked three miles every day*"). ¶Ducrot and Todorov 1979; Greimas and Courtés 1982; Todorov 1981.

predictive narrative. A narrative in which the NARRATION precedes the NARRATED in time; a narrative characterized by ANTERIOR NARRATION: "You will kill your father, and you will marry your mother." ¶Genette 1980; Todorov 1969.

primary narrative. A narrative the NARRATING INSTANCE of which introduces one (or more than one) other narrating instance and is not itself introduced by any: in *Manon Lescaut,* for example, M. de Renoncourt's narrative is primary, while Des Grieux's is "secondary." Of course, a primary narrative is not necessarily more important or interesting than the one(s) it introduces; indeed, the opposite is often true *(Manon Lescaut, Canterbury Tales).* ¶Genette 1980, 1983; Rimmon 1976. See also DIEGETIC LEVEL, EMBEDDING, EXTRADIEGETIC, VOICE.

prior narrating. A NARRATING that precedes the situations and events narrated, an AN-

TERIOR NARRATION. ¶Genette 1980. See also PREDICTIVE NARRATIVE.

privilege. A narrator's special right or ability. The narrator may be more or less privileged in knowing what cannot be known by strictly "natural" means: for example, an OMNISCIENT NARRATOR has complete privilege. ¶Booth 1983; Chatman 1978; Prince 1982. See also AUTHORITY.

proairetic code. The CODE, or "voice," according to which a narrative or part thereof can be structured as a series of ACTION sequences which themselves can be combined into larger sequences, etc.; the code regulating the folding of actions into larger actions or their unfolding into smaller ones; the code governing the construction of PLOT. ¶A passage can signify in terms of the proairetic code if it introduces (integral elements of) an initial situation to be modified in the world of the NARRATED, or if it presents activities (which may combine into larger activities) modifying the (modified) initial situation, or if it reports activities causing, resulting from, or pertinent to the modifying activities, or if it recounts (integral elements of) a modified situation. ¶Barthes 1974, 1981a; Culler 1975; Prince 1982.

proairetism. A unit of the PROAIRETIC CODE. ¶Barthes 1974.

problem. A situation making the fulfillment of a GOAL (or SUBGOAL) uncertain. The term is often used in artificial intelligence–inspired accounts of narrative structure. ¶Beaugrande 1980.

process. The transformation from one state to another. A two-state process constitutes a simple or minimal process (and is analo-gous to a MINIMAL STORY). An n-state process (where $n > 2$) constitutes a complex process. ¶Genot 1979.

process statement. A NARRATIVE STATEMENT in the mode of *do* or *happen;* a statement presenting an EVENT and, more specifically, an ACT or a HAPPENING. Along with the STASIS STATEMENT, it is one of two kinds of statements with which the DISCOURSE states the STORY. ¶Chatman 1978.

prolepsis. An ANACHRONY going forward to the future with respect to the "present" moment; an evocation of one or more events that will occur after the "present" moment (or moment when the chronological recounting of a sequence of events is interrupted to make room for the prolepsis); an ANTICIPATION, a FLASHFORWARD, a PROSPECTION: "John became furious. A few days later, he would come to regret his attitude, but now, he did not think of the consequences and he began to scream." ¶Prolepses have a certain EXTENT, or AMPLITUDE (they cover a certain amount of STORY TIME), as well as a certain REACH (the story time they cover is at a certain temporal distance from the "present" moment): in "Mary did not seem to notice it. Yet, the day after, she would think about it for several hours," the prolepsis has an extent of several hours and a reach of one day. ¶Completing prolepses fill in later gaps resulting from ELLIPSES in the narrative. Repeating prolepses, or ADVANCE NOTICES, recount ahead of time events that will be recounted again. ¶Genette 1980; Rimmon 1976. See also ANALEPSIS, ORDER.

prologue. An initial section in some narratives, preceding and not including the EXPOSITION or (part of) the COMPLICATION. ¶Tomashevsky 1965. See also EPILOGUE.

prop. An EXISTENT that is not active in the situations and events recounted. As opposed to a PARTICIPANT, a prop constitutes part of the SETTING. ¶Grimes 1975.

proposition. An elementary story unit constituted by a subject and a PREDICATE; a MOTIF. Propositions describe states ("X is Y") or events ("X does Y"). Some are logically essential to the narrative action and its causal-chronological coherence, whereas others are not. They combine into SEQUENCES and can be related temporally, spatially, causally, transformationally, and so on. ¶Todorov 1981. See also TRANSFORMATION.

prospection. An ANTICIPATION, a FLASHFORWARD, a PROLEPSIS. ¶Todorov 1981. See also ANACHRONY, ORDER.

protagonist. The main CHARACTER; the character constituting the chief focus of interest. A narrative articulated in terms of an interpersonal CONFLICT involves two major characters with opposite goals: the protagonist (or the HERO) and the ANTAGONIST. ¶N. Friedman 1975; Frye 1957; Tomashevsky 1965. See also ANTIHERO, SUBJECT.

pseudodiegetic narrative. A SECOND-DEGREE NARRATIVE brought up to the level of the PRIMARY NARRATIVE and taken in charge by its narrator; a METADIEGETIC NARRATIVE functioning as if it were a DIEGETIC one: if, in *Manon Lescaut,* M. de Renoncourt, after des Grieux had told him the story of his love for Manon, proceeded to narrate that story as if another narrator had not recounted it to him, a pseudodiegetic or REDUCED METADIEGETIC NARRATIVE would obtain. ¶Genette 1980. See also DIEGETIC LEVEL.

pseudo-iterative frequency. A type of FREQUENCY whereby events that (presumably) could have happened only once are recounted iteratively, as if they had happened many times. ¶Genette 1980. See also ITERATIVE NARRATIVE.

psychonarration. A NARRATIZED DISCOURSE representing a character's thoughts (as opposed to utterances), in the context of THIRD-PERSON NARRATIVE; INTERNAL ANALYSIS. ¶Cohn distinguishes three basic techniques for rendering consciousness: psychonarration (the most indirect one), NARRATED MONOLOGUE, and QUOTED MONOLOGUE (the most direct one). ¶Cohn 1966, 1978. See also SELF-NARRATION.

qualification. **1.** In Greimas's early model of narrative, a static PREDICATE (as opposed to the FUNCTION, or dynamic predicate). **2.** The consequence of the QUALIFYING TEST in Greimas's account of the canonical NARRATIVE SCHEMA. Qualification corresponds to the SUBJECT's acquisition of COMPETENCE along the axes of ability (being able to do or be) and/or knowledge (knowing how to do or be).

¶Greimas 1970, 1983a, 1983b; Greimas and Courtés 1982; Hénault 1983.

qualifying test. One of the three fundamental TESTS characterizing the movement of the SUBJECT in the canonical NARRATIVE SCHEMA. Presupposed by the DECISIVE TEST, which is in turn presupposed by the GLORIFYING TEST, the qualifying test results in the Subject's QUALIFICATION. ¶Greimas 1970, 1983b; Greimas and Courtés 1982; Hénault 1983.

quasi-direct discourse. See FREE INDIRECT DISCOURSE. ¶Vološinov 1973.

quasi-direct speech. QUASI-DIRECT DISCOURSE, especially quasi-direct discourse whereby a character's utterances (as opposed to thoughts) are represented; FREE INDIRECT SPEECH. ¶Bakhtin 1981.

quest. The figuration, at the discursive level, of the movement of the desiring SUBJECT toward the OBJECT desired. The goal of a quest is the CONJUNCTION of Subject and Object. ¶Greimas 1970, 1983a, 1983b; Greimas and Courtés 1982; Hénault 1983.

quoted monologue. A verbatim quotation of a character's mental language, in the context of THIRD-PERSON NARRATIVE; an INTERIOR MONOLOGUE; a REPORTED DISCOURSE representing a character's thoughts (as opposed to utterances). ¶Cohn distinguishes three basic techniques for rendering consciousness: quoted monologue (the most direct one), NARRATED MONOLOGUE, and PSYCHONARRATION (the most indirect one). ¶Cohn 1966, 1978. See also AUTONOMOUS MONOLOGUE, DIRECT DISCOURSE, SELF-QUOTED MONOLOGUE.

ravelling. COMPLICATION; COMPLICATING ACTION; MIDDLE (as opposed to BEGINNING or END). ¶Brooks and Warren 1959. See also UNRAVELLING.

reach. The temporal distance between the STORY TIME covered by an ANACHRONY and the "present" moment (or moment when the chronological recounting of a sequence of events is interrupted to make room for the anachrony). ¶Genette 1980.

reader. The decoder or interpreter (of a written narrative). This real or concrete reader is not to be confused with the IMPLIED READER of a narrative or with its NARRATEE and, unlike them, is not immanent to or deducible from the narrative. *Heart of Darkness* and *Vipers' Tangle,* for example, have different implied readers as well as different narratees, but they can have the same real reader. Furthermore, a narrative with only one implied reader and only one narratee ("The Wall") can have two or more real readers. ¶Booth 1983; Chatman 1978; Eco 1979; Prince 1982; Rabinowitz 1977.

readerly text. A text that can be read (or decoded) in terms of well-defined constraints, conventions, and codes; a text adapted to (more or less established) reading strategies. The readerly text *(texte lisible)* is a moderately polysemous text, a parsimoniously plural text, a partially closed text, as opposed to the WRITERLY TEXT *(texte scriptible),* which is infinitely polysemous, triumphantly plural, perfectly open. Narrative texts are readerly if only because they signify in terms of a logic of action (the PROAIRETIC CODE and its various constraints). ¶Barthes 1974.

reality effect. A seemingly functionless detail presumably reported just "because it is there (in the world of the NARRATED)," a detail presumably mentioned for no other reason than the fact that it is part of the reality represented. Reality effects *(effets de réel)* are exemplary connotators of the real (they signify "this is real"), and an abundance of them characterizes realistic narrative. ¶Barthes 1982.

recall. A repeating ANALEPSIS; an analepsis telling anew already mentioned past events. ¶Genette 1980. See also RETURN.

receiver. **1.** An ACTANT or fundamental ROLE at the level of deep narrative structure, in the Greimassian model. The Receiver (analogous to Souriau's EARTH) is the one who (eventually) receives the OB-JECT looked for by the SUBJECT. **2.** An ADDRESSEE. A distinction is sometimes made between the addressee and the mere receiver (who may not be the AD-DRESSER's intended addressee). ¶Greimas 1970, 1983b; Greimas and Courtés 1982; Hénault 1983. See also ACTANTIAL MODEL.

recognition. In Aristotelian terminology, a change from ignorance to knowledge experienced by a PROTAGONIST, brought about by the events in the PLOT and resulting in a turning of the action. ¶According to Aristotle, recognition (DISCOVERY, ANAGNORISIS) is, along with PERIPETY (PERIPETEIA, REVERSAL), the most potent means of securing the tragic effect. Furthermore, it is

most effective when closely allied to peripety. ¶Aristotle 1968.

recounted discourse. See NARRATIZED DISCOURSE. ¶Todorov 1981.

reduced metadiegetic narrative. See PSEUDODIEGETIC NARRATIVE. ¶Genette 1980.

referent. See CONTEXT. ¶Jakobson 1960.

referential code. The CODE, or "voice," in terms of which a narrative or part thereof refers to a given cultural background, to various stereotypic bodies of knowledge (physical, psychological, literary, artistic, philosophic, historic, medical, etc.) and cultural objects. ¶An important function of the referential code is to activate models of what is *vraisemblable* (verisimilar, lifelike). ¶Barthes 1974, 1981a. See also CULTURAL CODE, VERISIMILITUDE.

referential function. One of the FUNCTIONS OF COMMUNICATION in terms of which any communicative (verbal) act may be structured and oriented; the REPRESENTATIVE FUNCTION. When the communicative act is centered on the REFERENT or CONTEXT (rather than on one of the other CONSTITUTIVE FACTORS OF COMMUNICATION), it (primarily) has a referential function: "John is intelligent and handsome." More specifically, those passages in a narrative mainly focusing on (this or that feature of) the situations and events narrated can be said to fulfill a referential function. ¶Jakobson 1960; Prince 1982.

reflector. In Jamesian terminology, the FOCALIZER, the FOCUS OF NARRATION, the holder of POINT OF VIEW, the CENTRAL CONSCIOUSNESS or CENTRAL INTELLIGENCE. ¶H. James 1972. See also FOCALIZATION.

reliable narrator. A NARRATOR behaving in

accordance with the IMPLIED AUTHOR'S norms. Mike Hammer, in *I, The Jury,* is a reliable narrator. ¶Booth 1983. See also UNRELIABLE NARRATOR.

repeating narrative. A narrative or part thereof with a FREQUENCY such that what happens once is recounted *n* times (with or without stylistic variations): "At two o'clock Mary saw Nancy! At two o'clock Mary saw Nancy! She felt really good." ¶Genette 1980.

reportability. The quality that makes situations and events reportable, worthy of being told. Situations and events that are (shown to be) extraordinary, wonderful, bizarre (as opposed to ordinary, commonplace, humdrum), are reportable. ¶A reportable assertion can be said to have the force of an exclamatory one, and narrators usually underline the reportability (TELLABILITY) of their assertions through evaluative devices. ¶Labov 1972; Pratt 1977. See also EVALUATION, NARRATABLE.

reported discourse. DIRECT DISCOURSE. Along with TRANSPOSED DISCOURSE (INDIRECT DISCOURSE) and NARRATIZED DISCOURSE, reported discourse is, in Genette's view, one of the three basic ways of representing characters' utterances and verbal thoughts. ¶Reported discourse is formally distinguished from IMMEDIATE DISCOURSE (FREE DIRECT DISCOURSE) by the presence of a TAG CLAUSE (or some other form of narratorial mediation) introducing the characters' words or thoughts. ¶Genette 1980, 1983. See also TYPES OF DISCOURSE.

reported speech. REPORTED DISCOURSE, especially reported discourse whereby a character's utterances (as opposed to thoughts) are represented. ¶Genette 1980, 1983. See also DIALOGUE, DIRECT SPEECH.

representation. SHOWING, in Todorov's terminology: representation is to NARRATION as showing is to TELLING. ¶Todorov 1966.

representative function. The REFERENTIAL FUNCTION. ¶K. Bühler 1934. See also CONSTITUTIVE FACTORS OF COMMUNICATION, FUNCTIONS OF COMMUNICATION.

represented perception. A TYPE OF DISCOURSE whereby the narrator, instead of presenting the external world, presents a character's perceptions of it, presumably as they occur in his or her consciousness and without suggesting that the character has verbalized them. Whereas "—Here comes Mary, said John" would constitute a speech about perception rather than a transcription of perception and whereas "John saw Mary coming toward him" would constitute a report about perception, "John just stood there. Mary was coming toward him" provides an example of represented perception (substitutionary perception, *style indirect libre de perception, erlebte Wahrnehmung, erlebte Eindrück*). ¶Banfield 1982; Brinton 1980; W. Bühler 1937; Fehr 1938; Lips 1926. See also FREE INDIRECT DISCOURSE.

represented speech and thought. See FREE INDIRECT DISCOURSE. ¶Banfield 1982.

resolution. **1.** In Aristotelian terminology, that part of the plot which goes from the beginning of the change in fortune to the END. In that sense, resolution *(lusis)* should not be confused with DENOUEMENT. **2.** See RESULT. ¶Aristotle 1968; Labov 1972.

resolved content. The thematic situation resulting from the TRANSFORMATION of its contrary (or contradictory) and marking the completion of a narrative SEQUENCE. ¶Narrative can be viewed as correlating a temporal opposition (before / after, initial situation / final situation) and a thematic one (INVERTED CONTENT / resolved content). ¶Chabrol 1973; Greimas 1970; Rastier 1973.

restricted clause. A clause the DISPLACE-MENT SET of which is greater than that of a NARRATIVE CLAUSE but smaller than that of a FREE CLAUSE. A restricted clause can be displaced over a large part of the narrative without any resulting change in the semantic interpretation, but it cannot be displaced over the entire narrative: in "It was five o'clock. The birds started to sing. At ten past five, Mary got up," "It was five o'clock" is a restricted clause. ¶Labov 1972; Labov and Waletzky 1967. See also COORDINATE CLAUSES.

restriction of field. The subjecting of POINT OF VIEW to conceptual or perceptual constraints. ¶Blin 1954. See also FOCALIZATION, LIMITED POINT OF VIEW.

result. In Labov's terminology, the outcome of the events constituting the COMPLICATING ACTION; the END. If a NARRATIVE is taken to constitute a series of answers to certain questions, the result, or RESOLUTION, is that constituent of it answering the question "What finally happened?" ¶In a "fully developed" narrative, the resolution is followed by a CODA. ¶Labov 1972.

retrospection. An ANALEPSIS, a FLASHBACK, a CUTBACK, a SWITCHBACK. ¶Todorov 1981. See also ANACHRONY, ORDER.

return. A completing ANALEPSIS; an analepsis filling in a gap resulting from an earlier

ELLIPSIS in the narrative. ¶Genette 1980. See also RECALL.

reversal. See PERIPETY.

rewrite rule. A rule of the form X→Y (to be read "Rewrite X as Y" or "X consists of Y") and allowing for the replacement of a given element in a string by one or several other elements. For example, the fact that a sentence consists of a noun phrase and a verb phrase would be captured by a rule such as Sentence→Noun Phrase + Verb Phrase (the symbol + indicates the combination of elements in sequential order); similarly, the fact that a MINIMAL STORY consists of one event following a state of affairs obtaining at time t_0 and preceding another state of affairs obtaining at time t_1 would be captured by a rule such as Minimal Story→State at t_0 + Event + State at t_1. ¶Rewrite rules were imported into NARRATOLOGY from generative grammar, and they play an important part in STORY GRAMMARS. ¶Chomsky 1957, 1962; Pavel 1985; Prince 1973, 1982; Thorndyke 1977. See also NARRATIVE GRAMMAR, TRANSFORMATIONAL RULE.

rhythm. A recurrent pattern in narrative SPEED and, more generally, any pattern of repetition with variations. The most common rhythm in classical narrative results from the regular alternation of SCENE and SUMMARY. ¶Brown 1950; Genette 1980; T. Wright 1985.

rising action. Along with the FALLING ACTION and the CLIMAX, one of the fundamental constituents of a (dramatic or closely knit) PLOT structure. The rising action proceeds from the EXPOSITION and culminates in the climax. ¶Freytag 1894. See also FREYTAG'S PYRAMID.

role. A typical set of FUNCTIONS performable by and ATTRIBUTES attachable to an entity. ¶There have been several typologies of roles proposed, of which some have proven particularly influential in NARRATOLOGY. Thus, Propp isolated seven DRAMATIS PERSONAE, or basic functional roles, in his account of the structure of the fairy tale, each corresponding to a certain SPHERE OF ACTION: the VILLAIN, the DONOR (provider), the HELPER, the princess (a SOUGHT-FOR PERSON) and her father, the DISPATCHER, the HERO, and the FALSE HERO. ¶Souriau distinguished six basic roles, or dramatic functions: the LION (the Oriented Thematic Force, the SUBJECT, the HERO), the SUN (the Representative of the desired OBJECT, of the orienting value), the EARTH (the potential Obtainer of this Object, the one for whose benefit the Oriented Thematic Force is ultimately working, the RECEIVER), MARS (the OPPONENT), the BALANCE (the arbiter or rewarder, the attributor of the good, the imparter of values, the SENDER), and the MOON (the rescuer, the helper). ¶Greimas devised an ACTANTIAL MODEL representing the structure of relationships obtaining among ACTANTS, or fundamental roles, at the level of deep narrative structure. The original model involved six actants: Subject, Object, Sender, Receiver, Helper, and Opponent. In a more recent version of the model, the Helper and the Opponent no longer constitute actants. ¶Bremond developed an intricate typology by making a fundamental distinction between PATIENTS (victims or beneficiaries) and AGENTS (influencers, modifiers, and maintainers). ¶One role can be fulfilled by several different ACTORS or CHARACTERS, and conversely, one actor or character can fulfill several different roles. ¶Bremond 1973; Ducrot and Todorov 1979, Greimas 1970, 1983a, 1983b; Greimas and Courtés 1982; Propp 1968; Scholes 1974; Souriau 1950. See also STOCK CHARACTER, TYPE.

round character. A complex, multidimensional, unpredictable CHARACTER, who is capable of convincingly surprising behavior. Charlus in *Remembrance of Things Past* is a round character. ¶Forster 1927. See also FLAT CHARACTER.

S

sanction. In the Greimassian account of canonical narrative structure, that part of the action whereby the SUBJECT who has fulfilled (failed to fulfill) a CONTRACT is (justly) rewarded or (unjustly) punished by the SENDER. ¶Adam 1984, 1985; Greimas 1970, 1983a; Greimas and Courtés 1982. See also GLORIFYING TEST, NARRATIVE SCHEMA.

satellite. A FREE MOTIF; a CATALYSIS; a minor plot event. As opposed to KERNELS, satellites are not logically essential to the narrative action, and their elimination does not destroy its causal-chronological coherence: rather than constituting crucial nodes in the action, they fill in the narrative space between these nodes. ¶Barthes 1975; Chatman 1978. See also FUNCTION.

scale. The relative amount of detail used to represent a particular set of situations and events; the length of a narrative (or part thereof) relative to the situations and events recounted. ¶Brooks and Warren 1959. See also DURATION, SPEED.

scene. A canonical narrative TEMPO; along with ELLIPSIS, PAUSE, STRETCH, and SUMMARY, one of the fundamental narrative SPEEDS. When there is some sort of equivalence between a narrative segment and the NARRATED it represents (as in DIALOGUE, for instance), when the DISCOURSE TIME is (considered) equal to the STORY TIME, scene obtains. ¶The conventional equivalence between narrative segment and narrated is usually marked (in English) by the (relative) absence of narratorial mediation, the emphasis on moment-by-moment action, the careful detailing of specific events, the use of the preterit rather than the imperfect, the preference for point-action verbs rather than durational ones, etc. ¶Scene (DRAMA) is traditionally contrasted with summary (PANORAMA). ¶Chatman 1978; Genette 1980; Prince 1982. See also DURATION, RHYTHM.

schema. A global semantic framework representing various aspects of reality and guiding perception and comprehension of these (or related) aspects (Bartlett). ¶Schemata are often taken to be equivalent to FRAMES, PLANS, and SCRIPTS, but certain suggestive distinctions have been proposed: a schema is a serially ordered, temporally bound frame (a "house" schema, for instance, would represent the order in which houses are built or else the order in which people visit or inspect them); a plan in a goal-directed schema; and a script is a stereotypical plan. ¶Bartlett 1932; Beaugrande 1980.

script. A representation of knowledge the elements of which are viewed as instructions about the proper fulfillment of certain roles (Schank and Abelson). A "restaurant" script, for example, contains instructions for the customer, the waiter, the cashier, and so on. ¶Though scripts are frequently considered equivalent to FRAMES, PLANS, and SCHEMATA, they are more properly described as stereotypical, goal-directed schemata. ¶Beaugrande 1980; Schank and Abelson 1977.

second-degree narrative. See METADIEGETIC NARRATIVE. ¶Genette 1980, 1983.

second-person narrative. A narrative the NARRATEE of which is the PROTAGONIST in the story s/he is told. Butor's *A Change of Heart* is a second-person narrative. ¶Genette 1983; Morrissette 1965; Prince 1982. See also PERSON.

selective omniscience. One of eight possible POINTS OF VIEW according to Friedman's classification: selective omniscience characterizes the HETERODIEGETIC NARRATOR adopting FIXED INTERNAL FOCALIZATION *(A Portrait of the Artist as a Young Man).* ¶N. Friedman 1955b. See also MULTIPLE SELECTIVE OMNISCIENCE.

self-conscious narrator. A NARRATOR who is aware that s/he is narrating; a narrator who discusses and comments on his or her narrating chores. Jacques Revel in *Passing Time* and Holden Caulfield in *The Catcher in the Rye* are self-conscious narrators; Meursault in *The Stranger* and the narrator in "Haircut" are not. ¶Booth 1983.

self-narrated monologue. A NARRATED MONOLOGUE in a FIRST-PERSON NARRATIVE. ¶Cohn 1978. See also FREE INDIRECT DISCOURSE.

self-narration. A PSYCHONARRATION in a FIRST-PERSON NARRATIVE. ¶Cohn 1978.

self-quoted monologue. A QUOTED MONOLOGUE in a FIRST-PERSON NARRATIVE. ¶Cohn 1978.

self-reflexive narrative. A narrative taking itself and/or those narrative elements by which it is constituted and communicated (NARRATOR, NARRATEE, NARRATION, etc.) as a subject of reflection. *Tristram Shandy* and *Passing Time* are self-reflexive narratives; *I, the Jury* and *Germinal* are not. ¶Chambers 1984; Dällenbach 1977; Hutcheon 1984.

seme. **1.** An elementary semantic feature (Greimas); a minimal unit of meaning. The meaning of the word *colt,* for example, is the product of such semes as 'equine', 'young', 'male', etc. **2.** A unit of the SEMIC CODE (Barthes); a connotative SIGNIFIED; an element connoting a certain character (or setting) trait. Given a male character who has long eyelashes and a soft voice and who bites and scratches when he fights, the length of the eyelashes, the softness of the voice, and the biting and scratching can be said to function as semes of femininity. ¶Barthes 1974; Chatman 1978; Culler 1975; Greimas 1983b; Greimas and Courtés 1982; Rastier 1973.

sememe. **1.** The set of SEMES recognizable in a given word or morpheme (Pottier). **2.** A particular acceptation of a given word (Greimas). The word *bachelor,* for instance, brings together several sememes, since it means "young knight," "one who has received the first academic degree conferred by a college or university," "a man who has not married," "a male animal without a mate during the breeding time," etc. ¶Greimas 1983b; Greimas and Courtés 1982; Pottier 1964; Rastier 1973.

semic code. The CODE, or "voice," in terms of which a narrative or part thereof allows for the construction of CHARACTERS (and SETTINGS). ¶Barthes 1974, 1981a. See also SEME.

semiotic square. The visual representation of the logical articulation of any semantic category or, in other words, the visual representation of the CONSTITUTIVE MODEL describing the elementary structure of signification. In the Greimassian model, given a unit of sense s_1 (e.g., rich), it signifies in terms of relations with its contradictory $\overline{s_1}$ (not rich), its contrary s_2 (poor), and the contradictory of s_2 ($\overline{s_2}$, not poor):

where

$\longleftrightarrow$: relation of contradiction

$\leftarrow$ - - $\rightarrow$: relation of contrariety

$\longrightarrow$: relation of complementarity

($\overline{s_1}$ and $\overline{s_2}$ imply s_1 and s_2 respectively). ¶According to Greimas, the (semantic) course of a narrative can be said to correspond to a movement along the semiotic square: the narrative deploys itself in terms of operations (transformations) leading from a given unit to its contrary (or contradictory). For instance, the course of "John was *full of life.* One day, he became very sick and fell into such a *deep coma* that he was thought to be *dead.* But something in him *refused to die,* and he was miraculously restored to *normal life*" could be represented by the following diagram (to be read following the direction of the arrows and starting from A):

Similarly, the course of (Perrault's) "Cinderella," in which (1) the heroine finds herself *in a state that is not rightly hers* (she has lost her favorable position after her widowed father's remarriage); (2) with the help of a fairy, she *appears* as a beautiful lady at a ball; (3) on the stroke of midnight, she *no longer has that appearance;* and (4) she is *recognized by the prince for the worthy person she really is,* could be represented by the following diagram (starting from A):

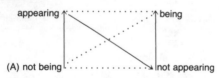

¶Adam 1984, 1985; Bremond 1973; Greimas 1970, 1983b; Greimas and Courtés 1982.

sender. **1.** An ACTANT or fundamental ROLE at the level of deep narrative structure, in the Greimassian model. The Sender (analogous to Souriau's BALANCE and Propp's DISPATCHER) is the imparter of values and sends the SUBJECT on its quest for the OBJECT. **2.** An ADDRESSER. ¶Greimas 1970, 1983a, 1983b; Greimas and Courtés 1982; Hénault 1983. See also ACTANTIAL MODEL, ANTISENDER.

sequence. A component unit of NARRATIVE that is itself capable of functioning as a narrative; a series of situations and events of which the last one in time constitutes a partial repetition or TRANSFORM of the first one. In "Jane was happy, and Susan was unhappy; then Susan met Flora, and she became happy; then Jane met Peter, and she became unhappy," "Susan was unhappy; then Susan met Flora, and she became happy" constitutes a sequence and so does "Jane was happy; then Jane met Peter, and she became unhappy." The combination of sequences through LINKING, EMBEDDING, and ALTERNATION yields ever more COMPLEX STORIES. ¶An elementary sequence—or (Bremond) TRIAD—is made up of three terms or FUNCTIONS corresponding to the three stages in any process: virtuality (situation opening a possibility), actualization of possibility, and result. ¶Barthes 1975; Bremond 1973; Ducrot and Todorov 1979; Greimas 1970, 1971, 1983b; Greimas and Courtés 1982; Prince 1982; Todorov 1981. See also PROPOSITION, TRANSFORMATION.

set description. A DESCRIPTION that is not developed in terms of a character's POINT OF VIEW or actions. ¶Chatman 1978.

setting. The spatiotemporal circumstances in which the events of a narrative occur. ¶Setting may be textually prominent or negligible, consistent (when its features are not contradictory) or inconsistent, vague or precise, presented objectively or subjectively, presented in an orderly fashion (the facade of a house is described from left to right, a door is depicted from top to bottom, a castle is shown from the inside to the outside, or vice versa) or in a disorderly one, and so on. Furthermore, it can be utilitarian (every part of it has a function in the action), symbolic (of a conflict to come, of a character's feelings), "irrelevant" ("realistic": it is presented simply because it is there, as it were), and so forth. Finally, its features may be introduced contiguously (a DESCRIPTION can then be said to obtain) or scattered one by one through the narrative. ¶Chatman 1978; Grimes 1975; Hamon 1981, 1982; Liddell 1947; Prince 1982. See also EXISTENT, REALITY EFFECT, SPACE.

shifter. A term or expression whose referent is determinable only with respect to the situation (ADDRESSER, ADDRESSEE, time, place) of its utterance (Jakobson): "I" and "Dad" are shifters. ¶Benveniste 1971; Ducrot and Todorov 1979; Jakobson 1971.

showing. Along with TELLING, one of two fundamental kinds of DISTANCE regulating narrative information; MIMESIS. ¶As opposed to telling or DIEGESIS *(diégésis),* showing is a MODE characterized by the detailed, scenic rendering of situations and events and by minimal narratorial mediation: DIALOGUE constitutes a good example of showing. ¶Chatman 1978; Genette 1980, 1983; H. James 1972; Lubbock 1965. See also SCENE.

sign. 1. In Saussurean terminology, a socially constituted entity linking a perceptible image (or SIGNIFIER) and a concept (or SIGNIFIED) neither of which exists outside of its relation with the other. The sign *dog,* for instance, links a series of visible marks with the concept "dog." 2. An entity standing for another entity. ¶Saussure 1966.

signified. The conceptual dimension of a SIGN. A signified *(signifié)* is linked with a SIGNIFIER *(signifiant)* and does not exist outside of its relation with it. ¶Saussure 1966.

signifier. The perceptual dimension of a SIGN. A signifier *(signifiant)* is linked with a SIGNIFIED *(signifié)* and does not exist as such outside of its relation with it. ¶Saussure 1966.

simultaneism. The concurrent rendering, through intercutting and INTERWEAVING, of two or more sets of situations and events occurring simultaneously *(The Reprieve, Manhattan Transfer,* the *U.S.A.* trilogy). ¶Beach 1932; Magny 1972.

simultaneous narrating. A NARRATING that is simultaneous with the situations and events narrated; a SIMULTANEOUS NARRATION. ¶Genette 1980.

simultaneous narration. A NARRATION contemporaneous with the situations and events narrated; a SIMULTANEOUS NARRATING *(The Unnameable).* ¶Prince 1982.

singulative narrative. A narrative or part thereof with a FREQUENCY such that what happened once is recounted once (or what happened *n* times is recounted *n* times): "At ten past six, Mary got up and left." ¶Genette 1980.

singular narrative. See SINGULATIVE NARRATIVE. ¶Genette 1980.

sjužet. In Russian formalist terminology, the set of narrated situations and events in the order of their presentation to the receiver (as opposed to FABULA); the arrangement of incidents; MYTHOS; PLOT. ¶Chatman 1978; Ejxenbaum 1971b; Erlich 1965.

skaz. A narrative devised as specifically oral

in terms of style; a narrative fashioned to give the illusion of spontaneous speech. *Skaz* (from Russian *skazat'*/*skazyvat'*, "to tell, relate") is told in language that is typical of the fictional NARRATOR (as opposed to the AUTHOR) and is firmly set in a communication framework. The manner of telling (the distinctive features and peculiarities of the narrator's speech) is as important to the effect of the narrative as the situations and events recounted. "Haircut" and *Huckleberry Finn* would be examples of *skaz,* whereas *Robinson Crusoe* and *David Copperfield* would not. ¶Bakhtin 1984; Banfield 1982; Lemon and Reis 1965; Titunik 1963; Vinogradov 1980.

slow motion. A cinematic manifestation of STRETCH (cf. Peckinpah's *The Wild Bunch* or Penn's *Bonnie and Clyde*). With slow motion, an action takes less time than its representation, which proceeds at less than usual speed. ¶Chatman 1978.

sought-for person. One of the seven fundamental ROLES that a character may assume (in a fairy tale), according to Propp. The sought-for person (analogous to Souriau's SUN and Greimas's OBJECT) is usually represented by a princess. ¶Propp 1968. See also ACTANT, DRAMATIS PERSONA, SPHERE OF ACTION.

space. The place or places within which the situations and events represented (SETTING, story space) and the NARRATING INSTANCE(S) occur. ¶Though it is possible to narrate without referring to the story space, the space of the narrating instance, or the relations between them ("John ate; then he slept"), space can play an important role in narrative; and the features of or links between the above-mentioned places can be significant and function thematically, structurally, or as a CHARACTERIZATION device. Should a narrator narrate from a hospital bed, for instance, it may mean that s/he is near death and has to rush in order to complete the NARRATION. Furthermore, one can easily conceive of narratives in which the space of the narrating instance is systematically constrasted with that of the NARRATED (I narrate from a prison cell events that took place in wide-open spaces); or narratives in which the former is progressively more (or less) distant and different from the latter and in which, consequently, the narration is more (or less) precise (I start narrating in Philadelphia events occurring in New York; I continue my narration in Princeton; and I finish it in New York); or narratives in which the various places where the events narrated occur are represented in more or less detail, according to different points of view; and so on. ¶Bal 1977, 1985; Bonheim 1982; Bourneuf and Ouellet 1975; Chatman 1978; Hamon 1981, 1982; Prince 1982; Zoran 1984. See also DESCRIPTION.

spatial form. An arrangement obtaining in narrative when the usual logico-temporal modes of narrative organization are abandoned in favor of modes traditionally privileged by (nonnarrative) poetry. With spatial form, the temporal movement of an episode stops; attention is drawn to relations of symmetry, antithesis, gradation, repetition, etc., between the episode constituents, and meaning springs from these relations, as in the country-fair scene in *Madame Bovary.* ¶Frank 1945.

specification. The rhythm of recurrence of the event or set of events in an ITERATIVE NARRATIVE. In "John took a shower once a week" the series has a specification of one day out of seven. ¶Specification can be indefinite ("John *often* took a cold shower") or definite ("John took a cold shower *every Monday*"). It can also be simple ("Mary went to the movies *every other day*") or complex (when two or more patterns of recurrence are combined "*Every summer, on Sundays,* Mary went to the movies"). ¶Genette 1980.

speech act. An utterance considered as a goal-directed act. The performance of a speech act involves that of a LOCUTIONARY ACT (an act of saying, of producing a grammatical utterance), that of an ILLOCUTIONARY ACT (performed *in* saying something, to accomplish some purpose: make a promise, an assertion, a request, give a warning, issue a command, etc.), and (possibly) that of a PERLOCUTIONARY ACT (performed *by means of* saying something and describable in terms of the effect which the illocutionary act, on the particular occasion of use, has on the ADDRESSEE: persuading someone to do something, convincing someone that something is the case, etc.). For example, uttering "I promise to be there" in a given context involves the locutionary act of making a sentence according to the rules of English, the illocutionary act of promising, and (possibly) the perlocutionary act of convincing the addressee of one's good faith. In the case of so-called indirect speech acts, an illocutionary act is performed indirectly by way of the performance of another illocutionary

act. Thus, taken literally, "I wish you would open the window" is an assertion about the ADDRESSER's feelings; yet, in particular contexts, it can (and does) perform the illocutionary act of making a request. ¶The theory of speech acts originates in J. L. Austin's distinction between CONSTATIVES (utterances like "Napoleon won the battle of Austerlitz" or "The earth is flat" that report events or states of affairs in certain worlds and, consequently, are either true or false in these worlds) and PERFORMATIVES (utterances like "I promise to come" or "I now pronounce you husband and wife" that are used to do rather than to say something, to perform an act rather than to state that something is or is not the case). However, as Austin goes on to argue, constatives are themselves performatives, since saying (asserting, stating, reporting) that something is or is not the case constitutes a kind of doing. Indeed, any utterance or set of utterances can be viewed as performative and can be regarded as a speech act. ¶NARRATIVE can, of course, be taken to constitute a speech act, a kind of complex or global one subsuming the more local ones of the narrator(s) and the character(s). ¶Austin 1962; Chatman 1978; van Dijk 1977; Lanser 1981; Lyons 1977; Pratt 1977; Searle 1969, 1975, 1976.

speed. The relationship between the duration of the NARRATED—the (approximate) amount of time (presumably) covered by the situations and events recounted—and the length of the narrative (in words, lines, or pages, for example). ¶Narrative speed can vary considerably and its canonical forms—the major narrative TEMPOS—are (in descending order, from infinity to zero) ELLIPSIS, SUMMARY, SCENE, STRETCH, and PAUSE. ¶Genette 1980; Prince 1982. See also ANISOCHRONY, DURATION, RHYTHM.

sphere of action. The set of FUNCTIONS corresponding to a particular ROLE or DRAMATIS PERSONA (Propp). Seven spheres of action can be distinguished: (1) the sphere of action of the VILLAIN: villainy, struggle, pursuit; (2) the sphere of action of the DONOR: first function of the donor (preparation for the transmission of a magical agent), provision of a magical agent; (3) the sphere of action of the HELPER: spatial transference of the hero, liquidation of misfortune or lack, rescue, solution, transfiguration; (4) the sphere of action of a princess (a SOUGHT-FOR PERSON) and her father: branding, difficult task, exposure, recognition, punishment, wedding (the princess and her father are not easy to distinguish from each other in terms of functions; usually, it is the father who proposes difficult tasks to the HERO and who punishes the FALSE HERO, and it is the princess who marries the hero); (5) the sphere of action of the DISPATCHER: mediation; (6) the sphere of action of the hero: departure, reaction, wedding (the first function—departure on a search—is distinctive of the hero as seeker rather than of the hero as victim); (7) the sphere of action of the FALSE HERO: departure, reaction, and—specific to the false hero—unfounded claims. ¶A sphere of action may correspond exactly to one CHARACTER or be distributed among several characters. Conversely, one character may be involved in several spheres of action. ¶Propp 1968. See also ACTANT.

stance. The relation between the NARRATOR and the NARRATED. Along with CONTACT and STATUS, stance is one of three basic relations in terms of which POINT OF VIEW is structured. ¶Lanser 1981.

stasis statement. A NARRATIVE STATEMENT in the mode of *is,* one presenting a STATE and, more specifically, establishing the existence of entities by identifying them or qualifying them (cf. "Mary was an engineer" and "Mary was happy"). Along with the PROCESS STATEMENT, it is one of two kinds of statements with which the DISCOURSE states the STORY. ¶Chatman 1978.

state. The condition of a system (or part thereof) at a given point of operation; a set of elements characterized by a number of properties and relations at a given time or place; a situation. NARRATIVE is the representation of one or more changes of state. ¶Beaugrande 1980; van Dijk 1974–75; Genot 1979. See also EVENT, MOTIF, STASIS STATEMENT.

status. The relation between the NARRATOR and the act of NARRATING. Along with CONTACT and STANCE, status is one of three basic relations in terms of which POINT OF VIEW is structured. ¶Lanser 1981.

stock character. A conventional CHARACTER traditionally associated with a given (narrative) genre or form; a TYPE. The cruel stepmother and the prince charming are stock characters in fairy tales. ¶Holman 1972.

stock situation. A conventional situation; a

standard set of states and events. Stock situations go from the particular (e.g., the birthmark that reveals kinship) to the general (e.g., the rags-to-riches kind of PLOT). Some are considered to be more archetypal than merely conventional (e.g., the death and rebirth kind of story). ¶Holman 1972.

story. 1. The CONTENT plane of NARRATIVE as opposed to its EXPRESSION plane or DISCOURSE; the "what" of a narrative as opposed to its "how"; the NARRATED as opposed to the NARRATING; the FICTION as opposed to the NARRATION (in Ricardou's sense of the terms); the EXISTENTS and EVENTS represented in a narrative. 2. The FABULA (or basic material arranged into a PLOT) as opposed to the SJUŽET or plot. 3. A narrative of events with an emphasis on chronology, as opposed to plot, which is a narrative of events with an emphasis on causality (Forster): "The king died, and then the queen died" is a story, whereas "The king died, and then the queen died of grief" is a plot. 4. A causal sequence of events pertinent to a character or characters seeking to solve a problem or reach a goal. As such, though every story is a narrative (the recounting of one or more events), not every narrative is necessarily a story (consider, for instance, a narrative merely recounting a temporal sequence of events that are not causally related). 5. According to Benveniste, and along with discourse (DISCOURS), one of two distinct and complementary linguistic subsystems. Whereas discourse involves some reference to the situation of enunciation and implies a SENDER and a RECEIVER, story or history (HISTOIRE) does not. Compare "He has eaten" or "I've reminded you of it many times" with "He ate" or "She reminded him of it many times." ¶Benveniste's distinction between *histoire* and *discours* is analogous to Weinrich's distinction between ERZÄHLTE WELT and BESPROCHENE WELT and reminiscent of Hamburger's distinction between FIKTIONALE ERZÄHLEN and AUSSAGE. ¶Beaugrande 1980; Benveniste 1971; Chatman 1978; Doležel 1976; Forster 1927; Genette 1980; Prince 1973, 1982; Shklovsky 1965b; Stein 1982; Tomashevsky 1965. See also COMPLEX STORY, MINIMAL STORY.

story grammar. A grammar or series of statements and formulas interrelated by an ordered set or rules and accounting for (the structure of) a set of STORIES; a grammar specifying the "natural" constituents of (a set of) stories and characterizing their relations. ¶Story grammars take a story to consist of a series of EPISODES which bring a CHARACTER closer to or farther from a GOAL through the reaching or not reaching of a SUBGOAL. In the grammar for simple stories devised by Thorndyke, for instance, each rule in the ordered set is of the form $X \rightarrow Y$ (to be read "Rewrite X and Y" or "X consists of Y"); parentheses are used to enclose optionally chosen items; different possible rewritings of the same item or different items that yield the same rewriting are listed within braces; an asterisk (*) indicates that an element may be repeated; and the symbol + indicates the combination of elements in sequential order:

(1) Story→ Setting + Theme + Plot + Resolution

(2) Setting→ Characters + Location + Time

(3) Theme→ (Event)* + Goal

(4) Plot→ Episode*

(5) Episode→ Subgoal + Attempt* + Outcome

(6) Attempt→ $\begin{Bmatrix} \text{Event*} \\ \text{Episode} \end{Bmatrix}$

(7) Outcome→ $\begin{Bmatrix} \text{Event*} \\ \text{State} \end{Bmatrix}$

(8) Resolution→ $\begin{Bmatrix} \text{Event} \\ \text{State} \end{Bmatrix}$

(9) $\begin{Bmatrix} \text{Subgoal} \\ \text{Goal} \end{Bmatrix}$ → Desired State

(10) $\begin{Bmatrix} \text{Characters} \\ \text{Location} \\ \text{Time} \end{Bmatrix}$ → State

¶Developed by students of cognitive psychology and artificial intelligence, story grammars have influenced decisively the study of the effects of structure and content variables on memory and the comprehension of narrative texts: they are attempts to capture the abstract structural schemes allowing for the retention and understanding of narrative. ¶Black and Bower 1980; van Dijk 1980; Glenn 1978; Mandler and Johnson 1977; Rumelhart 1975; Schank 1975; Thorndyke 1975; Wilensky 1978. See also NARRATIVE GRAMMAR, REWRITE RULE.

story-line. The set of events in a story that involve the same individuals. In *The Reprieve,* for example, the events involving Milan Hlinka and his wife Anna constitute one story-line and the events involving Ma- thieu and his acquaintances or relations constitute another one. In many narratives, a predominant or main story-line can be distinguished from subsidiary ones. ¶Rimmon-Kenan 1983.

story time. The period of time in which the NARRATED occurs; ERZÄHLTE ZEIT. ¶Chatman 1978. See also DISCOURSE TIME, DURATION.

stream of consciousness. A kind of FREE DIRECT DISCOURSE or INTERIOR MONOLOGUE attempting to give "a direct quotation of the mind" (Bowling); a mode of representation of human consciousness focusing on the random flow of thought and stressing its illogical, "ungrammatical," associative nature (Molly Bloom's monologue in *Ulysses*). ¶Though interior monologue and stream of consciousness have often been considered interchangeable, they have also frequently been contrasted: the former would present a character's thoughts rather than impressions or perceptions, while the latter would present both impressions and thoughts; or else, the former would respect morphology and syntax, whereas the latter would not (punctuation is then absent, grammatical forms truncated, short incomplete sentences numerous, neologisms frequent) and would thus capture thought in its nascent stage, prior to any logical connection. ¶The term was coined by William James to describe the way consciousness presents itself. ¶Bowling 1950; Chatman 1978; Cohn 1978; M. Friedman 1955; Genette 1980; Humphrey 1954; W. James 1890; Scholes and Kellogg 1966.

stretch. A canonical narrative TEMPO (Chatman); along with ELLIPSIS, PAUSE, SCENE, and SUMMARY, one of the fundamental narrative SPEEDS. When DISCOURSE TIME is (taken to be) greater than STORY TIME, when a narrative segment is (felt to be) too lengthy for the NARRATED it represents, when a relatively long (part of the) narrative text corresponds to a relatively short narrated time (to a narrated action that is usually completed in a short time), stretch obtains ("Occurrence at Owl Creek Bridge"). ¶If summary covers the range of speeds between scene and ellipsis, stretch covers the range of speeds between pause and scene. ¶Chatman 1978; Genette 1980; Prince 1982. See also DURATION, SLOW MOTION.

structural analysis of narrative. The analysis of narrative in terms of its STRUCTURE. In accounting for (a given) narrative, structural analysis gives priority to (syntactico-semantic) relations (as opposed to, say, origin, function, or substance). ¶Barthes 1975.

structure. The network of relations obtaining between the various constituents of a whole as well as between each constituent and the whole. Should narrative be defined as consisting of STORY and DISCOURSE, for example, its structure would be the network of relations obtaining between story and discourse, story and narrative, and discourse and narrative. ¶Chatman 1978; Greimas and Courtés 1982; Piaget 1980.

style indirect libre. See FREE INDIRECT DISCOURSE. ¶Bally 1912.

subgoal. An intermediate STATE in a (character's) plan to reach a desired GOAL. ¶Beaugrande 1980; Black and Bower 1980; Rumelhart 1975; Thorndyke 1975. See also STORY GRAMMAR.

subject. An ACTANT or fundamental ROLE at the level of deep narrative structure, in the Greimassian model. The SUBJECT (analogous to Propp's HERO and Souriau's LION) looks for the OBJECT. At the level of narrative surface structure, it is concretized as the PROTAGONIST. ¶Greimas 1970, 1983a, 1983b; Greimas and Courtés 1982; Hénault 1983. See also ACTANTIAL MODEL, ACTANTIAL ROLE, ANTISUBJECT, AUXILIANT, NARRATIVE SCHEMA, NARRATIVE TRAJECTORY.

subjective narrative. **1.** A narrative characterized by an OVERT NARRATOR whose feelings, beliefs, and judgments color the treatment of the situations and events presented. **2.** A narrative in which the thoughts or feelings of one or more characters are presented (as opposed to BEHAVIORIST NARRATIVE). ¶Brooks and Warren 1959. See also OBJECTIVE NARRATIVE.

subplot. A unified set of actions coincident with but subordinate to the (main) PLOT. ¶Souvage 1965. See also DOUBLE PLOT.

subsequent narrating. A narrating that follows the situations and events narrated; a POSTERIOR NARRATION. Subsequent narrating is characteristic of most narratives. ¶Genette 1980.

substance. Following Hjelmslev, and as opposed to FORM, the (material or semantic) reality constitutive of the two planes of a semiotic system (the EXPRESSION plane and the CONTENT plane). ¶In the case of narrative, the substance of the expression can be said to be equivalent to the medium of narrative MANIFESTATION (language, film, etc.) and the substance of the content to the set of possible entities and events that can be represented by a narrative. ¶Chatman 1978; Ducrot and Todorov 1979; Hjelmslev 1954, 1961. See also DISCOURSE, NARRATIVE MEDIUM, STORY.

substitutionary narration. See FREE INDIRECT DISCOURSE. ¶Fehr 1938; Hernadi 1972.

summary. A canonical narrative TEMPO; along with ELLIPSIS, PAUSE, SCENE, and STRETCH, one of the fundamental narrative SPEEDS. When DISCOURSE TIME is (taken to be) smaller than STORY TIME, when a narrative segment is (felt to be) too brief for the NARRATED it represents, when a relatively short (part of the) narrative text corresponds to a relatively long narrated time (to a narrated action that it usually takes a long time to complete), summary obtains: it covers the range of speeds between scene and ellipsis. ¶Summary (or PANORAMA) is traditionally contrasted with scene (or DRAMA) and, in classical narrative, constitutes the connective between scenes as well as the background against which they come to the fore. ¶Bentley 1946; Chatman 1978; Genette 1980; Prince 1982. See also DURATION, RHYTHM.

sun. One of six fundamental ROLES or FUNCTIONS isolated by Souriau (in his study of the possibilities of drama). The Sun (analogous to Greimas's OBJECT and Propp's SOUGHT-FOR PERSON) is the representation of the desired object and orients the action of the LION. ¶Scholes 1974; Souriau 1950. See also ACTANT.

surface structure. The particular way the deep or underlying structure of a narrative is realized: surface structure is related to DEEP STRUCTURE by a set of operations or TRANSFORMATIONS; the MICROSTRUCTURE of narrative. In the Greimassian model of narrative, for example, whereas ACTANTS and actantial relations would be elements of the deep structure, ACTORS and actorial relations would be found at the surface structure level. In other models of narrative, whereas the deep structure might be said to correspond to STORY, the surface structure might be said to correspond to DISCOURSE (or the stating of the story). ¶The term and concept were adapted from Chomsky and generative-transformational grammar. ¶Chomsky 1965; van Dijk 1972; Johnson and Mandler 1980. See also NARRATIVE GRAMMAR.

surprise. The emotion obtaining when expectations about what is going to happen are violated by what in fact does happen. The production of surprise is considered particularly effective when, although what in fact does happen violates expectations, it is well grounded in what happened earlier. ¶The interplay of surprise and SUSPENSE traditionally constitutes an important feature of good plotting. ¶Chatman 1978.

suspense. An emotion or state of mind arising from a partial and anxious uncertainty about the progression or outcome of an action, especially one involving a positive character. Suspense obtains, for instance, when a certain result is possible but whether it will actually come to pass is not clear or when a given outcome is known but how and when it will occur is not. ¶Suspense often depends on FORESHAD-

OWING and, more generally, on the thematizations, snares, and suspended answers structured in terms of the HERME-NEUTIC CODE. ¶Bal 1985; Barthes 1974; Chatman 1978; Rabkin 1973; Sternberg 1978. See also HERMENEUTEME, SURPRISE.

switchback. An ANALEPSIS; a FLASHBACK; a RETROSPECTION; a CUTBACK. ¶Souvage 1965. See also ANACHRONY, ORDER.

syllepsis. A grouping of situations and events governed by a nonchronological principle (spatial, thematic, etc.) rather than by a chronological one. In "He remembered that time very well. He had drunk huge amounts of cola; he had dated a lot; and he had read a little," the representation of the events remembered constitutes a syllepsis. ¶Genette 1980. See also ORDER.

symbolic code. The CODE, or "voice," in terms of which a narrative or part thereof can acquire a symbolic dimension; the code governing the production/reception of symbolic meaning. Given a series of antithetical terms in a text, they can—through associations and extrapolations regulated by the symbolic code—be taken to represent more abstract, fundamental, and general oppositions and meanings. ¶Barthes 1974, 1981a.

synchronic analysis. The study of a (linguistic) system as it appears at one and the same moment (without bringing into play factors or elements belonging to other moments). ¶Saussure 1966. See also DIACHRONIC ANALYSIS.

syntagm. A rule-governed sequence of two or more units of the same type. In "Jane blushed," the words "Jane" and "blushed" form a syntagm and so do the sounds /dž/, /eI/, and /n/ whereas the word "Jane" and the sound /b/ do not. ¶In an early version of the Greimassian model of narrative, three types of fundamental narrative syntagms were identified: performative (relating to tests and struggles), contractual (pertaining to the establishing and breaking of contracts), and disjunctional (involving various kinds of movements and displacements, of departures and returns). ¶Ducrot and Todorov 1979; Greimas 1970; Greimas and Courtés 1982; Saussure 1966. See also PARADIGM.

T

tag. See TAG CLAUSE. ¶Chatman 1978.

tag clause. A clause ("he said," "she thought," "she asked," "he replied") accompanying a character's discourse (speech or verbalized thought) and specifying the act of the speaker or thinker, identifying him or her, and (sometimes) indicating various aspects of the act, the character, the setting in which they appear, etc. ¶Tag clauses (or TAGS) can accompany DIRECT DISCOURSE ("—What are you doing here? he asked with a smile") or INDIRECT DISCOURSE ("She said that she was exhausted"). In ABRUPTIVE DIALOGUE as well as in FREE DIRECT DISCOURSE and FREE INDIRECT DISCOURSE (excepting parentheticals and as opposed to TAGGED INDIRECT DISCOURSE), no tag clauses accompany the utterance or thought.

¶Chatman 1978; Page 1973; Prince 1978. See also ATTRIBUTIVE DISCOURSE, INQUIT FORMULA, VERBUM DICENDI.

tagged direct discourse. A DIRECT DISCOURSE accompanied by a TAG CLAUSE. ¶Chatman 1978.

tagged indirect discourse. An INDIRECT DISCOURSE accompanied by a TAG CLAUSE. ¶Chatman 1978.

tellability. See REPORTABILITY.

telling. Along with SHOWING, one of two fundamental kinds of DISTANCE regulating narrative information; DIEGESIS (*diégésis*). ¶Telling is a MODE characterized by more narratorial mediation and a less detailed rendering of situations and events than SHOWING (or MIMESIS): NARRATIZED DISCOURSE constitutes a good example of telling. ¶Chatman 1978; Genette 1980, 1983; H. James 1972; Lubbock 1965.

tempo. A rate of narrative SPEED. ELLIPSIS, SUMMARY, SCENE, STRETCH, and PAUSE are the five major tempos in narrative. ¶Bentley 1946; Chatman 1978; Genette 1980.

temporal juncture. The temporal separation obtaining between two NARRATIVE CLAUSES. Given a sequence of temporally ordered clauses, the displacement of clauses across a temporal juncture leads to a change in the semantic interpretation of the original sequence: compare "John had lunch; then John went to bed" and "John went to bed; then John had lunch." ¶For Labov, a MINIMAL NARRATIVE is one containing a single temporal juncture. ¶Labov 1972; Labov and Waletzky 1967.

tense. 1. The set of temporal relations—SPEED, ORDER, DISTANCE, etc.—between the situations and events recounted and their recounting, STORY and DISCOURSE,

NARRATED and NARRATING. 2. In grammar, a form indicative of a time distinction. Psychologists, linguists, and students of fiction and literature (Bühler, Benveniste, Weinrich) have frequently argued that tenses can be grouped in two main categories: tenses related to the DEICTIC system of "I-here-now," to the situation of ENUNCIATION (e.g., the present perfect—"he has eaten"—which connects a past occurrence with the present time), and tenses not related to it (e.g., the preterite—"he ate"—which refers to a past occurrence without connecting it to the present time). Narrative privileges the members of the second group (e.g., the preterite but also the imperfect and the pluperfect, as opposed to the present, the present perfect, and the future). ¶Benveniste 1971; Bronzwaer 1970; K. Bühler 1934; Ducrot and Todorov 1979; Genette 1980; Todorov 1966; Weinrich 1964. See also BESPROCHENE WELT, EPIC PRETERITE, ERZÄHLTE WELT.

test. A narrative SYNTAGM characterizing the movement of the SUBJECT toward its goal and involving a polemical or transactional confrontation (a struggle for a given object or an exchange of objects), a domination (by the Subject), and its consequence. ¶In the canonical NARRATIVE SCHEMA developed by Greimas and his school, the Subject undergoes a QUALIFYING TEST, a DECISIVE TEST, and a GLORIFYING TEST. ¶Adam 1984; Greimas 1970, 1983a, 1983b; Greimas and Courtés 1982; Hénault 1983; Larivaille 1974.

thematic role. A set of attributes and behaviors which, in conjunction with at least one ACTANTIAL ROLE, defines an ACTOR. There are professional roles (the physician, the teacher, the farmer, the priest, etc.), familial ones (the father, the stepmother, the older brother, etc.), psychosocial ones (the pedant, the snob, the paranoiac, etc.), and so on. ¶In the Greimassian model of narrative, the thematic role constitutes an intermediate category between ACTANT and actor: it helps to specify the former and is in turn specified by the latter. ¶Greimas 1983a; Greimas and Courtés 1982; Hamon 1972, 1983; Hénault 1983.

theme. A semantic macrostructural category or FRAME extractable from (or allowing for the unification of) distinct (and discontinuous) textual elements which (are taken to) illustrate it and expressing the more general and abstract entities (ideas, thoughts, etc.) that a text or part thereof is (or may be considered to be) about. ¶A theme should be distinguished from other kinds of macrostructural categories or frames that also connect or allow for the connecting of textual elements and express what a text or segment thereof is (partly) about: it is an "idea" frame rather than, for example, an action frame (PLOT) or an existent frame (CHARACTER, SETTING). ¶Moreover, a theme should be distinguished from a MOTIF, which is a more concrete and specific unit manifesting it, and from a TOPOS, which is constituted (rather than illustrated) by a specific complex of motifs. ¶Finally, the theme of a work could be distinguished from its THESIS (the doctrine it supports). Unlike the latter, the former does not promote an answer but helps to raise questions: it is contemplative rather than assertive. ¶Barthes 1974; Beardsley 1958; Bremond 1985; Chatman 1983; van Dijk 1977; Daemmrich and Daemmrich 1986;

Ducrot and Todorov 1979; Falk 1967; N. Friedman 1975; Frye 1957; Prince 1985; Rimmon-Kenan 1985; Wellek and Warren 1949; Zholkovsky 1984.

thesis. The doctrine or ideological context of a text; the (philosophical, moral, political) views advanced by that text. The thesis of a work could be distinguished from its THEME: it promotes an answer instead of raising questions and asks to be agreed with rather than thought about. Thus, the theme of a given novel might be the decline of Southern aristocracy whereas its thesis might be that this decline was most regrettable. ¶Beardsley 1958; Chatman 1983; Suleiman 1983.

third-person narrative. A narrative whose narrator is not a character in the situations and events recounted; a HETERODIEGETIC NARRATIVE; a narrative that "is about" third persons ("he," "she," "they"). "He was happy; then he lost his job, and he became unhappy" is a third-person narrative, and so are *Sons and Lovers, The Trial,* and *One Hundred Years of Solitude.* ¶Genette 1983; Prince 1982. See also PERSON.

thought. **1.** Along with CHARACTER (ETHOS), one of two fundamental qualities that an AGENT (or PRATTON) has, according to Aristotle. Thought (DIANOIA) is an agent's vision of the world, an agent's conception of things; it is revealed by his or her emotions, beliefs, statements, and reasonings. **2.** The THEME or, more generally, the meaning of a literary work, according to Frye. In narrative, thought (*dianoia*) can be viewed as the MYTHOS in stasis (and *mythos* would be *dianoia* in movement) ¶Aristotle 1968; N. Friedman 1975; Frye 1957.

time. The period or periods during which the situations and events presented (STORY TIME, time of the NARRATED, ERZÄHLTE ZEIT) and their presentation (DISCOURSE TIME, time of the NARRATING, ERZÄHLZEIT) occur. ¶Chatman 1978; Mendilow 1952; Metz 1974; Müller 1968; Prince 1982. See also DURATION, SPEED, TENSE.

tone. The narrator's attitude toward the NARRATEE and/or the situations and events presented, as implicitly or explicitly conveyed by his or her narration. ¶Tone can be taken to be a function of DISTANCE. ¶Brooks and Warren 1959; Richards 1950.

topos. Any of a stable disposition of MOTIFS that frequently appears in (literary) texts. Such *topoï* as those of the wise fool, the aged child, and the *locus amoenus* are very common in Western literature ¶Curtius 1973; Ducrot and Todorov 1979. See also THEME.

trait. A CHARACTER's quality or feature that recurs in a series of situations and events. ¶Chatman 1978. See also ATTRIBUTE, SEME.

transform. The string resulting from the application of a TRANSFORMATION to a certain (set of) string(s). Given a string of situations and events "A—then—B—then—C," for example, "C—before C—A—then—B" could be said to be a transform of it, resulting from the application of an order transformation to the original string (cf. "She had been poor; then she won the lottery; then she became rich" and "She became rich. Before she became rich, she had been poor, then she won the lottery"). ¶The term *transform* was borrowed from generative-transformational grammar. ¶Prince 1973.

See also TRANSFORMATIONAL RULE.

transformation. An operation relating two strings or two structural levels within the same text or two (strings within) different texts. ¶According to Todorov, for example, a transformation is a relation obtaining between two PROPOSITIONS that have a PREDICATE in common, and it can be simple (involving the addition of an operator—of modality, negation, etc.—to a base predicate: "X eats a hamburger every day" → "X does not eat a hamburger every day") or complex (involving the grafting of a predicate onto a base predicate: "X eats a hamburger every day" → "X [or Y] says that X eats a hamburger every day"). Among simple transformations, there are transformations of mode ("X must eat a hamburger every day"), intent ("X tries to eat a hamburger every day"), result ("X manages to eat a hamburger every day"), manner ("X hastens to eat a hamburger every day"), aspect ("X continues to eat a hamburger every day"), and status ("X does not eat a hamburger every day"). Among complex transformations, there are transformations of appearance ("X [or Y] claims that X eats a hamburger every day"), knowledge ("X [or Y] knows that X eats a hamburger every day"), description ("X [or Y] says that X eats a hamburger every day"), supposition ("X [or Y] suspects that X eats a hamburger every day"), subjectivization ("X [or Y] believes that X eats a hamburger every day"), and attitude ("X [or Y] likes the fact that X eats a hamburger every day"). For a narrative SEQUENCE to be complete, it must contain two distinct propositions in a transformational relation. ¶According to Greimas also, transformations link intratextual strings at the same structural level. They are equivalent to CONJUNCTION and DISJUNCTION operations between SUBJECT and OBJECT, and more generally, they lead from an initial state to a final one constituting its contrary or contradictory (its inversion or negation). ¶If, for Todorov and Greimas, transformations are intratextual and obtain at the same structural level, for some students of narrative—in particular, those who have been influenced by generative-transformational grammar (van Dijk, Pavel, Prince, etc.)—transformations are intratextual but (usually) relate two different structural levels (the underlying or DEEP STRUCTURE of a narrative and its SURFACE STRUCTURE). Specifically, they perform certain changes (permutations of elements, additions, deletions, etc.) in certain deep-structure strings (or their TRANSFORMS). For instance, given a string analyzable as "A—then—B—then—C," an order transformation operating on it might yield "C—before C—A—then—B," and a repetition transformation might yield "A—then—B—then—C—repeat A" (cf. "He had been very happy; then he left his hometown; then he became unhappy," "He became unhappy. Before he became unhappy, he had been very happy; then he left his hometown," and "He had been very happy; then he left his hometown; then he became unhappy. He had been very happy"). Two or more different surface structures might thus be derived form the same underlying structure. ¶On the other hand, some students of narrative (and, more particularly, of folktales and myths) take transformations to be intertextual rather than intratextual opera-

tions. According to Propp, for example, the specific actions concretizing the FUNCTIONS that constitute the fundamental components of any fairy tale can change from one tale (or set of tales) to another, and the changes (which may be considered to follow a historically determined evolution, with the marvelous becoming rational, for instance, or the heroic humoristic) are called transformations. Similarly, according to Lévi-Strauss, for whom a myth consists of all its versions, these versions can be said to be related by transformations. ¶Van Dijk 1980; Ducrot and Todorov 1979; Greimas 1970, 1971, 1983b; Greimas and Courtés 1982; Hénault 1983; Köngäs-Maranda and Maranda 1971; Lévi-Strauss 1963, 1965–71; Mandler and Johnson 1977; Pavel 1976, 1985; Prince 1973, 1982; Propp 1968, 1984; Todorov 1978, 1981. See also NARRATIVE GRAMMAR, TRANSFORMATIONAL RULE.

transformational rule. A rule allowing for the performance of certain changes in certain strings provided these strings have a certain structure. The first part of a transformational rule is a structural analysis (SA) specifying the kind of string to which the rule applies; the second part specifies the structural change (SC) by means of numbers referring to the elements in SA. For instance, to show that an event, A, can appear after another event, B, even though it precedes it in time (as in "She ate a hamburger; before that, she had eaten a pizza"), there might be a transformational rule such as:

SA: A—then—B

SC: 3—before 3—1

¶Transformational rules were imported into narratology from generative-transformational grammar and play an important role in some grammars of narrative. ¶Chomsky 1957, 1962, 1965; Prince 1973, 1982. See also NARRATIVE GRAMMAR, TRANSFORMATION.

transposed discourse. INDIRECT DISCOURSE. Along with REPORTED DISCOURSE (DIRECT DISCOURSE) and NARRATIZED DISCOURSE, transposed discourse is, in Genette's view, one of three basic ways of representing characters' utterances and verbal thoughts. ¶Genette 1980, 1983. See also TYPES OF DISCOURSE.

transposed speech. TRANSPOSED DISCOURSE, especially transposed discourse whereby a character's utterances (as opposed to thoughts) are represented. ¶Genette 1980, 1983. See also INDIRECT SPEECH.

trebling. See TRIPLICATION. ¶Propp 1968.

triad. A series of three units or FUNCTIONS corresponding to the three fundamental stages in the unfolding of any process—(1) virtuality (a situation's opening a possibility); (2) actualization or nonactualization of the possibility; (3) achievement or nonachievement—and constituting the elementary (minimal, atomic) narrative SEQUENCE:

$$\text{virtuality} \begin{cases} \text{actualization} \begin{cases} \text{achievement} \\ \text{nonachievement} \end{cases} \\ \text{nonactualization} \end{cases}$$

More specifically, a given elementary sequence might consist of "villainy, intervention of the hero, success," and another sequence might be made up of "villainy, intervention of the hero, failure." ¶Within a triad, a posterior term implies an anterior one but not vice versa: there is an intervention of the hero, for instance, only if there was a villainy, and there is a success only if there was an intervention. On the other hand, every anterior term offers a consequent alternative: a villainy might lead to an intervention or nonintervention of the hero, and an intervention might end in success or failure. ¶Triads can combine to yield more complex sequences, and according to Bremond, the most characteristic modes of combination are ENCHAINMENT ("back-to-back" succession, *bout à bout:* the outcome of one sequence constitutes the situation's opening a possibility in another sequence), EMBEDDING (*enclave:* one sequence is embedded into another and specifies or details one of its first two functions), and JOINING (*accolement:* the same sequence, considered from two different points of view, consists of two different sets of functions depending on the point of view adopted):

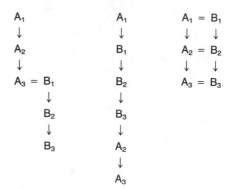

Bremond 1973, 1980.

triplication. The double repetition, at the level of the NARRATED, of one or more (sequences of) events; TREBLING. A character may, for instance, violate three interdictions or perform three difficult tasks. ¶Triplication is common in folk literature. ¶See also DUPLICATION.

turning point. The ACT or HAPPENING that is decisive in making a goal reachable or not. ¶Beaugrande 1980. See also CRISIS.

type. A static character whose attributes are very few and who constitutes a paradigm case of a given quality, attitude, or role (the miser, the braggart, the *femme fatale,* the hypochondriac, etc.) ¶Ducrot and Todorov 1979; Scholes and Kellogg 1966.

types of discourse. The basic modes of representation of a character's thoughts and (spoken or written) utterances. The following categories are usually distinguished on a scale of decreasing narratorial mediation: (1) NARRATIZED DISCOURSE; (2) TAGGED INDIRECT DISCOURSE (one variety of INDIRECT or TRANSPOSED DISCOURSE); (3) FREE INDIRECT DISCOURSE (another variety of indirect or transposed discourse); (4) (TAGGED) DIRECT DISCOURSE (REPORTED DISCOURSE); (5) FREE DIRECT DISCOURSE (IMMEDIATE DISCOURSE). ¶Chatman 1978; Genette 1980, 1983; McHale 1978; Rimmon-Kenan 1983.

U

undramatized narrator. A COVERT NARRATOR. ¶Booth 1983. See also DRAMATIZED NARRATOR.

unravelling. See DENOUEMENT. ¶See also RAVELLING.

unreliable narrator. A NARRATOR whose norms and behavior are not in accordance with the IMPLIED AUTHOR'S norms; a narrator whose values (tastes, judgments, moral sense) diverge from those of the implied author's; a narrator the reliability of whose account is undermined by various features of that account ("Haircut," *The Fall,* Hitchcock's *Stage Fright*). ¶Booth 1983; Chatman 1978. See also RELIABLE NARRATOR.

V

variable internal focalization. A type of INTERNAL FOCALIZATION or POINT OF VIEW whereby different FOCALIZERS are used in turn to present different situations and events (*The Age of Reason, The Golden Bowl*). ¶Genette 1980. See also FOCALIZATION.

variable internal point of view. See VARIABLE INTERNAL FOCALIZATION. ¶Prince 1982.

verbum dicendi. A verb that can appear in a TAG CLAUSE. *Verba dicendi* (literally, "verbs of saying") may occur with DIRECT or INDIRECT DISCOURSE and constitute a class that is usually taken to include not only verbs of linguistic communication ("say," "ask," "reply," "swear," "shout," etc.) but also verbs of belief, reflection, and emotion ("think," "believe," "feel," etc.) and, most generally, verbs that are viewed as specifying the act of the speaker or thinker ("—How are you? he smiled"). ¶Banfield, 1982; Page 1973; Prince 1978. See also ATTRIBUTIVE DISCOURSE, INQUIT FORMULA.

verisimilitude. The quality of a text resulting from its degree of conformity to a set of "truth" norms that are external to it: a text has (more or less) verisimilitude (gives more or less of an illusion of truth) depending on the extent to which it conforms to what is taken to be the case (to "reality") and to what is made suitable or expected by a particular generic tradition. ¶Culler 1975; Genette 1968; Todorov 1981. See also MOTIVATION, NATURALIZATION, REFERENTIAL CODE.

viewpoint. FOCALIZATION; POINT OF VIEW. Grimes distinguishes four basic categories: omniscient viewpoint (ZERO FOCALIZATION), first-person participant viewpoint (HOMODIEGETIC NARRATIVE with INTERNAL FOCALIZATION), third-person subjective viewpoint (HETERODIEGETIC NARRATIVE with internal focalization), and third-person objective viewpoint (EXTERNAL FOCALIZATION). ¶Grimes 1975.

viewpoint character. See FOCAL CHARACTER.

villain. 1. A wicked ANTAGONIST; an enemy of the hero, capable or guilty of evil doings. 2. One of the seven fundamental ROLES that a character may assume (in a fairy tale), according to Propp. The villain (analogous to Greimas's OPPONENT and Souriau's MARS) opposes the HERO and, more specifically, causes his misfortune or that of another character. ¶Propp 1968. See also ACTANT, DRAMATIS PERSONA, SPHERE OF ACTION.

vision. The POINT(S) OF VIEW in terms of which the narrated situations and events are presented. Pouillon devised a three-term categorization: (1) vision from behind (*vision par derrière,* analogous to ZERO FOCALIZATION or OMNISCIENT POINT OF VIEW; the narrator tells more than any and all of the characters know: *Tess of the D'Urbervilles*); (2) vision with (*vision avec,* analogous to INTERNAL FOCALIZATION; the narrator tells only what one or several characters know: *The Ambassadors, The Age of Reason*); and (3) vision from without (*vision du dehors,* analogous to EXTERNAL FOCALIZATION; the narrator tells less about certain situations and events than one or several characters know: "Hills Like White Elephants"). ¶Genette 1980; Pouillon 1946; Prince 1982; Todorov 1981. See also ASPECT.

voice. The set of signs characterizing the NARRATOR and, more generally, the NARRATING INSTANCE, and governing the relations between NARRATING and narrative text as well as between narrating and NARRATED. ¶Voice has a much larger extension than PERSON and, though often amalgamated or confused with POINT OF VIEW, should be distinguished from it: the latter provides information about who "sees," who perceives, whose point of view governs the narrative, whereas the former provides information about who "speaks," who the narrator is, what the narrating instance consists of. ¶Genette 1980, 1983; Rimmon 1976.

W

well-spoken narrator. A narrator whose mode of expression is a standard (or even elegant) one and functions as a norm in terms of which the characters' modes of expression are situated. ¶According to Hough, the contrast between the well-spoken narrator's diction and the characters' diction is characteristic of the novel as opposed to the epic. ¶Hough 1970.

writerly text. A text that cannot be read (or decoded) in terms of well-defined constraints, conventions, and codes; a text that is not adapted to (more or less) established decoding strategies; a text that is (to be) written rather than (already) read. The writerly text (*texte scriptible*) is a text signifying in infinitely many ways (in any and all ways). As opposed to the READERLY TEXT (*texte lisible*), it is triumphantly plural and totally open. ¶Strictly speaking, the term designates a (paradoxical) ideal and cannot characterize narrative texts, if only because they signify in terms of a logic of action (the PROAIRETIC CODE and its various constraints). Yet it has increasingly come to be used in connection with unconventional texts, including unconventional narratives. ¶Barthes 1974.

Z

zero focalization. A type of FOCALIZATION or POINT OF VIEW whereby the NARRATED is presented in terms of a nonlocatable, indeterminate perceptual or conceptual position. Zero focalization (or NONFOCALIZATION) is characteristic of "traditional" or "classical" narrative (*Vanity Fair, Eugénie Grandet*) and associated with OMNISCIENT NARRATORS. ¶Genette 1980. See also AUTHORIAL NARRATIVE SITUATION, OMNISCIENT POINT OF VIEW, VISION.

Bibliography

Adam, Jean-Michel. 1984. *Le Récit.* Paris: Presses Universitaires de France.

———. 1985. *Le Texte narratif.* Paris: Fernand Nathan.

Alexandrescu, Sorin. *Logique du personnage.* Tours: Mame.

Aristotle. 1968. *Poetics.* In *Aristotle's Poetics: A Translation and Commentary for Students of Literature.* Trans. Leon Golden. Commentary by O. B. Hardison, Jr. Englewood Cliffs, N.J.: Prentice Hall.

Arrivé, Michel. 1973. "Pour une théorie des textes poly-isotopiques." *Langages,* no. 31: 53–63.

Austin, J. L. 1962. *How to Do Things with Words.* New York: Oxford University Press.

Bakhtin, Mikhail. 1981. *The Dialogic Imagination.* Ed. Michael Holquist. Trans. Caryl Emerson and Michael Holquist. Austin: University of Texas Press.

———. 1984. *Problems of Dostoevsky's Poetics.* Ed. and trans. Caryl Emerson. Minneapolis: University of Minnesota Press.

Bal, Mieke. 1977. *Narratologie.* Paris: Klincksieck.

———. 1981a. "The Laughing Mice; or, On Focalization." *Poetics Today* 2:202–10.

———. 1981b. "Notes on Narrative Embedding." *Poetics Today* 2:41–59.

———. 1983. "The Narrating and the Focalizing: A Theory of the Agents in Narrative." *Style* 17:234–69.

———. 1985. *Narratology: Introduction to the Theory of Narrative.* Trans. Christine van Boheemen. Toronto: University of Toronto Press.

Bally, Charles. 1912. "Le Style indirect libre en français moderne." *Germanisch-romanische Monatsschrift* 4:549–56, 597–606.

Banfield, Ann. 1982. *Unspeakable Sentences: Narration and Representation in the Language of Fiction.* Boston: Routledge and Kegan Paul.

Barthes, Roland. 1968. *Writing Degree Zero.* Trans. Annette Lavers and Colin Smith. New York: Hill & Wang.

———. 1974. *S/Z.* Trans. Richard Miller. New York: Hill & Wang.

———. 1975. "An Introduction to the Structural Analysis of Narrative." *New Literary History* 6:237–62.

———. 1981a. "Textual Analysis of Poe's 'Valdemar.' " In Robert Young, ed., *Untying the Text: A Post-Structuralist Reader,* pp. 133–61. London: Routledge and Kegan Paul.

———. 1981b. "Theory of the Text." Ibid., pp. 31–47.

———. 1982. "The Reality Effect." In Tzvetan Todorov, ed., *French Literary Theory Today,* pp. 11–17. Trans. R. Carter.

Cambridge: Cambridge University Press, and Paris: Editions de la Maison des Sciences de l'Homme.

Bartlett, Frederic C. 1932. *Remembering: A Study in Experimental and Social Psychology.* New York: Macmillan.

Beach, Joseph Warren. 1932. *The Twentieth-Century Novel: Studies in Technique.* New York: Appleton-Century-Crofts.

Beardsley, Monroe. 1958. *Aesthetics: Problems in the Philosophy of Criticism.* New York: Harcourt, Brace.

Beaugrande, Robert de. 1980. *Text, Discourse, and Process: Toward a Multidisciplinary Science of Texts.* Norwood, N.J.: Ablex.

Benjamin, Walter. 1969. *Illuminations.* Trans. Harry Zohn. New York: Schocken Books.

Bentley, Phyllis. 1946. *Some Observations on the Art of Narrative.* London: Home & Van Thal.

Benveniste, Emile. 1971. *Problems in General Linguistics.* Trans. Mary Elizabeth Meek. Coral Gables, Fla.: University of Miami Press.

———. 1974. *Problèmes de linguistique générale. II.* Paris: Gallimard.

Berendsen, Marjet. 1981. "Formal Criteria of Narrative Embedding." *Journal of Literary Semantics* 10:79–94.

Bickerton, Derek. 1967. "Modes of Interior Monologue: A Formal Definition." *Modern Language Quarterly* 28:229–39.

Black, John B., and Gordon H. Bower. 1980. "Story Understanding as Problem-Solving." *Poetics* 9:223–50.

Blin, Georges. 1954. *Stendhal et les problèmes du roman.* Paris: Corti.

Bonheim, Helmut W. 1982. *The Narrative Modes: Techniques of the Short Story.* Cambridge, Eng.: D. S. Brewer.

Booth, Wayne C. 1961. "Distance and Point of View." *Essays in Criticism* 11:60–79.

———. 1983. *The Rhetoric of Fiction.* 2d ed. Chicago: University of Chicago Press.

Bourneuf, Roland, and Réal Ouellet. 1975. *L'Univers du roman.* Paris: Presses Universitaires de France.

Bowling, Lawrence E. 1950. "What Is the Stream of Consciousness Technique?" *PMLA* 55:333–45.

Bremond, Claude. 1973. *Logique du récit.* Paris: Seuil.

———. 1980. "The Logic of Narrative Possibilities." *New Literary History* 11:398–411.

———. 1982. "A Critique of the Motif." In Todorov, *French Literary Theory,* pp. 125–46. *See* Barthes, 1982.

———. 1985. "Concept et thème." *Poétique,* no. 64:415–23.

Brinton, Laurel. 1980. "'Represented Perception': A Study in Narrative Style." *Poetics* 10:363–81.

Bronzwaer, W.J.M. 1970. *Tense in the Novel: An Investigation of Some Potentialities of Linguistic Criticism.* Groningen: Wolters-Noordhoff.

———. 1978. "Implied Author, Extradiegetic Narrator, and Public Reader: Gérard Genette's Narratological Model and the Reading Version of *Great Expectations.*" *Neophilologus* 52:1–18.

Brooks, Cleanth, and Robert Penn Warren. 1959. *Understanding Fiction.* 2d ed. New York: Appleton-Century-Crofts.

Brooks, Peter. 1984. *Reading for the Plot:*

Design and Intention in Narrative. New York: A. A. Knopf.

Brown, E. K. 1950. *Rhythm in the Novel.* Toronto: University of Toronto Press.

Bruce, Bertram. 1978. "What Makes a Good Story?" *Language Arts* 55:460–66.

Bruce, Bertram, and Denis Newman. 1978. "Interacting Plans." *Cognitive Science* 2:195–233.

Bühler, Karl. 1934. *Sprachtheorie: Die Darstellungfunktion der Sprache.* Jena: Gustav Fischer.

Bühler, Willi. 1937. *Die 'erlebte Rede' im englischen Roman: Ihre Vorstufen und ihre Ausbildung im Werke Jane Austens.* Zurich: Max Niehaus Verlag.

Chabrol, Claude. 1973. "De quelques problèmes de grammaire narrative et textuelle." In Claude Chabrol, ed., *Sémiotique narrative et textuelle,* pp. 7–28. Paris: Larousse.

Chafe, Wallace, ed. 1980. *The Pear Stories: Cultural, Cognitive, and Linguistic Aspects of Narrative Production.* Norwood, N.J.: Ablex.

Chambers, Ross. 1984. *Story and Situation: Narrative Seduction and the Power of Fiction.* Minneapolis: University of Minnesota Press.

Chatman, Seymour. 1978. *Story and Discourse: Narrative Structure in Fiction and Film.* Ithaca: Cornell University Press.

———. 1983. "On the Notion of Theme in Narrative." In John Fisher, ed., *Essays in Aesthetics: Perspectives on the Work of Monroe C. Beardsley,* pp. 161–79. Philadelphia: Temple University Press.

Chomsky, Noam. 1957. *Syntactic Structures.* The Hague: Mouton.

———. 1962. "A Transformational Approach to Syntax." In A. A. Hill, ed., *Proceedings of the 1958 Conference on Problems of Linguistic Analysis in English,* pp. 124–58. Austin: University of Texas Press.

———. 1965. *Aspects of the Theory of Syntax.* Cambridge: MIT Press.

Clark, Katerina, and Michael Holquist. 1984. *Mikhaïl Bakhtin.* Cambridge: Harvard University Press.

Cohn, Dorrit. 1966. "Narrated Monologue: Definition of a Fictional Style." *Comparative Literature* 18:97–112.

———. 1978. *Transparent Minds: Narrative Modes for Presenting Consciousness in Fiction.* Princeton: Princeton University Press.

———. 1981. "The Encirclement of Narrative: On Franz Stanzel's *Theorie des Erzählens.*" *Poetics Today* 2:157–82.

Colby, Benjamin N. 1973. "A Partial Grammar of Eskimo Folktales." *American Anthropologist* 75:645–62.

Courtés, Joseph. 1976. *Introduction à la sémiotique narrative et discursive.* Paris: Hachette.

Crane, R. S. 1952. "The Concept of Plot and the Plot of *Tom Jones.*" In R. S. Crane, ed., *Critics and Criticism: Ancient and Modern,* pp. 616–47. Chicago: University of Chicago Press.

Culler, Jonathan. 1975. *Structuralist Poetics: Structuralism, Linguistics, and the Study of Literature.* Ithaca: Cornell University Press.

———. 1981. *The Pursuit of Signs: Semiotics, Literature, Deconstruction.* Ithaca: Cornell University Press.

Curtius, Ernst R. 1973. *European Literature*

and the Latin Middle Ages. Trans. Willard R. Trask. Princeton: Princeton University Press.

Daemmrich, Horst S., and Ingrid Daemmrich. 1986. *Themes and Motifs in Western Literature: A Handbook.* Tubingen: Francke.

Dällenbach, Lucien. 1977. *Le Récit spéculaire.* Paris: Seuil.

Danto, Arthur C. 1965. *Analytical Philosophy of History.* Cambridge: Harvard University Press.

Debray-Genette, Raymonde. 1980. "La Pierre descriptive." *Poétique,* no. 43: 293–304.

——. 1982. "Traversées de l'espace descriptif." *Poétique,* no. 51:359–68.

van Dijk, Teun A. 1972. *Some Aspects of Text Grammars: A Study in Theoretical Linguistics and Poetics.* The Hague: Mouton.

——. 1974–75. "Action, Action Description, and Narrative." *Poetics* 5:287–338.

——. 1976a. "Narrative Macro-Structures: Logical and Cognitive Foundations." *PTL* 1:547–68.

——. 1976b. "Philosophy of Action and Theory of Narrative." *Poetics* 5:287–338.

——. 1977. *Text and Context: Explorations in the Semantics and Pragmatics of Discourse.* London: Longman.

——. 1980. "Story Comprehension: An Introduction." *Poetics* 9:1–21.

Dillon, George, and Frederick Kirchhoff. 1976. "On the Form and Function of Free Indirect Style." *PTL* 1:431–40.

Doležel, Lubomír. 1972. "From Motifemes to Motifs." *Poetics,* no. 4:55–90.

——. 1973. *Narrative Modes in Czech Literature.* Toronto: Univeristy of Toronto Press.

——. 1976. "Narrative Semantics." *PTL* 1:129–51.

——. 1980. "Truth and Authenticity in Narrative." *Poetics Today* 1:7–25.

Dorfman, Eugene, 1968. *The Narreme in the Medieval Romance Epic: An Introduction to Narrative Structures.* Toronto: University of Toronto Press.

Ducrot, Oswald, and Tzvetan Todorov. 1979. *Encyclopedic Dictionary of the Sciences of Language.* Trans. Catherine Porter. Baltimore: Johns Hopkins University Press.

Dujardin, Edouard. 1931. *Le Monologue Intérieur.* Paris: Messein.

Dundes, Alan. 1962. "From Etic to Emic Units in the Structural Study of Folktales." *Journal of American Folklore* 75:95–105.

——. 1964. *The Morphology of North American Indian Folktales.* Helsinki: Suomalainen Tiedeakatemia.

Eco, Umberto. 1979. *The Role of the Reader.* Bloomington: Indiana University Press.

——. 1984. *Semiotics and the Theory of Language.* Bloomington: Indiana University Press.

Egan, Kieran. 1978. "What Is a Plot?" *New Literary History* 9:455–73.

Ejxenbaum, Boris M. 1971a. "O'Henry and the Theory of the Short Story." In Ladislav Matejka and Krystyna Pomorska, eds., *Readings in Russian Poetics,* pp. 227–70. Cambridge: MIT Press.

——. 1971b. "The Theory of the Formal Method." Ibid., pp. 3–37.

Empson, William. 1960. *Some Versions of Pastoral.* New York: New Directions.

Erlich, Victor. 1965. *Russian Formalism: His-*

tory, *Doctrine*. 2d ed. The Hague: Mouton.

Falk, Eugene H. 1965. *Types of Thematic Structure*. Chicago: Univeristy of Chicago Press.

Fehr, Bernhard. 1938. "Substitutionary Narration and Description: A Chapter in Stylistics." *English Studies* 20:97–107.

Forster, E. M. 1927. *Aspects of the Novel*. London: Methuen.

Francoeur, Louis. 1976. "Le Monologue intérieur narratif." *Etudes Littéraires* 9:341–65.

Frank, Joseph. 1945. "Spatial Form in Modern Literature." *Sewanee Review* 53:221–46, 433–56.

Freytag, Gustav. 1894. *Technique of the Drama*. Trans. E. J. McEwan. Chicago: Scott.

Friedemann, Käte. 1910. *Die Rolle des Erzählers in der Epik*. Leipzig: H. Haessel Verlag.

Friedman, Melvin. 1955. *Stream of Consciousness: A Study in Literary Method*. New Haven: Yale University Press.

Friedman, Norman. 1955a. "Forms of the Plot." *Journal of General Education* 8:241–53.

———. 1955b. "Point of View in Fiction: The Development of a Critical Concept." *PMLA* 70:1160–84.

———. 1975. *Form and Meaning in Fiction*. Athens: University of Georgia Press.

Frye, Northrop. 1957. *Anatomy of Criticism*. Princeton: Princeton University Press.

Füger, Wilhelm. 1972. "Zur Tiefenstruktur des Narrativen: Prolegomena zu einer generativen 'Grammatik' des Erzählens." *Poetica* 5:268–92.

Garvey, James. 1978. "Characterization in Narrative." *Poetics* 7:63–78.

Genette, Gérard. 1968. "Vraisemblance et motivation." *Communications*, no. 11: 5–21.

———. 1976. "Boundaries of Narrative." *New Literary History* 8:1–15.

———. 1980. *Narrative Discourse: An Essay in Method*. Trans. Jane E. Lewin. Ithaca: Cornell University Press.

———. 1982. *Palimpsestes: La Littérature au second degré*. Paris: Seuil.

———. 1983. *Nouveau Discours du récit*. Paris: Seuil.

Genot, Gérard. 1979. *Elements of Narrativics: Grammar in Narrative, Narrative in Grammar*. Hamburg: Helmut Buske Verlag.

———. 1984. *Grammaire et récit: Essai de linguistique textuelle*. Université Paris X—Nanterre: Documents du CRLLI 32.

Georges, Robert A. 1970. "Structure in Folktales: A Generative-Transformational Approach." *The Conch* 2:4–17.

Gibson, Walker. 1950. "Authors, Speakers, Readers, and Mock Readers." *College English* 11:265–69.

Glenn, Christine G. 1978. "The Role of Episodic Structure and Story Length in Children's Recall of Simple Stories." *Journal of Verbal Learning and Verbal Behavior* 17:229–47.

Głowiński, Michał. 1974. "Der Dialog im Roman." *Poetica* 8:1–16.

———. 1977. "On the First-Person Novel." *New Literary History* 9:103–14.

Goffman, Erving. 1974. *Frame Analysis: An Essay on the Organization of Experience*. Cambridge: Harvard University Press.

Greimas, A. J. 1970. *Du sens: Essais sémiotiques*. Paris: Seuil.

———. 1971. "Narrative Grammar: Units and Levels." *MLN* 86:793–806.

———. 1983a. *Du sens II: Essais sémiotiques.* Paris: Seuil.

———. 1983b. *Structural Semantics: An Attempt at a Method.* Trans. Daniele McDowell, Ronald Schleifer, and Alan Velie. Lincoln: University of Nebraska Press.

Greimas, A. J., and Joseph Courtés. 1976. "The Cognitive Dimension of Narrative Discourse." *New Literary History* 7:433–47.

———. 1982. *Semiotics and Language: An Analytical Dictionary.* Trans. Larry Crist et al. Bloomington: Indiana University Press.

Grimes, Joseph. 1975. *The Thread of Discourse.* The Hague: Mouton.

Hamburger, Käte. 1973. *The Logic of Literature.* Trans. Marilyn J. Rose. Bloomington: Indiana University Press.

Hamon, Philippe. 1972. "Pour un statut sémiologique du personnage." *Littérature,* no. 6:86–110

———. 1975. "Clausules." *Poétique,* no. 24:495–526.

———. 1977. "Texte littéraire et métalangage." *Poétique,* no. 31:261–84.

———. 1981. *Introduction à l'analyse du descriptif.* Paris: Hachette.

———. 1982. "What Is a Description?" In Todorov, *French Literary Theory,* pp. 147–78. *See* Barthes 1982.

———. 1983. *Le Personnel du roman.* Geneva: Droz.

Harvey, W. J. 1965. *Character and the Novel.* London: Chatto & Windus.

Hénault, Anne. 1983. *Narratologie: Sémiotique générale.* Paris: Presses Universitaires de France.

Hendricks, William O. 1973. *Essays on Semiolinguistics and Verbal Art.* The Hague: Mouton.

Hernadi, Paul. 1972. "Dual Perspective: Free Indirect Discourse and Related Techniques." *Comparative Literature* 24:32–43.

Hjelmslev, Louis. 1954. "La Stratification du langage." *Word* 10:163–88.

———. 1961. *Prolegomena to a Theory of Language.* Trans. Francis J. Whitfield. Madison: University of Wisconsin Press.

Hochman, Baruch. 1985. *Character in Literature.* Ithaca: Cornell University Press.

Holman, Hugh C. 1972. *A Handbook to Literature.* Based on the original by William Flint Thrall and Addison Hibbard. 3d ed. Indianapolis: Bobbs-Merrill.

Horace. 1974. *The Art of Poetry.* Trans. Burton Raffel. Albany: State University of New York Press.

Hough, Graham. 1970. "Narrative and Dialogue in Jane Austen." *Critical Quarterly* 12:201–29.

Humphrey, Robert. 1954. *Stream of Consciousness in the Modern Novel.* Berkeley and Los Angeles: University of California Press.

Hutcheon, Linda. 1984. *Narcissistic Narrative: The Metafictional Paradox.* London: Methuen.

———. 1985. *A Theory of Parody: The Teachings of Twentieth-Century Art Forms.* London: Methuen.

Hymes, Dell. 1970. "The Ethnography of Speaking." In Joshua A. Fishman, ed., *Readings in the Sociology of Language,* pp. 99–138. The Hague: Mouton.

Ingarden, Roman. 1973. *The Literary Work of Art*. Trans. George G. Grabowicz. Evanston: Northwestern University Press.

Iser, Wolfgang. 1974. *The Implied Reader: Patterns of Communication in Prose Fiction from Bunyan to Beckett*. Baltimore: Johns Hopkins University Press.

———. 1978. *The Act of Reading: A Theory of Aesthetic Response*. Baltimore: Johns Hopkins University Press.

Jakobson, Roman. 1956. "Two Aspects of Language and Two Types of Aphasic Disturbances." In Roman Jakobson and Morris Halle, *Fundamentals of Language*, pp. 53–82. The Hague: Mouton.

———. 1960. "Closing Statement: Linguistics and Poetics." In Thomas A. Sebeok, ed., *Style in Language*, pp. 350–77. New York: Wiley.

———. 1971. "Shifters, Verbal Categories, and the Russian Verb." In Roman Jakobson, *Selected Writings*, 2:130–47. The Hague: Mouton.

James, Henry. 1972. "The Art of Fiction, etc." In James E. Miller, Jr., ed., *Theory of Fiction: Henry James*. Lincoln: University of Nebraska Press.

James, William. 1890. *The Principles of Psychology*. 2 vols. New York: H. Holt.

Janik, Dieter. 1973. *Die Kommunikationstrucktur des Erzählwerks: Ein semiologisches Model*. Bebenhausen: Lothar Rotsch.

Jenny, Laurent. 1982. "The Strategy of Form." In Todorov, *French Literary Theory*, pp. 34–63. See Barthes 1982.

Jespersen, Otto. 1924. *The Philosophy of Grammar*. London: Allen & Unwin.

Johnson, Nancy S., and Jean M. Mandler. 1980. "A Tale of Two Structures: Underlying and Surface Forms in Stories." *Poetics* 9:87–98.

Jolles, André. 1956. *Einfache Formen*. Halle: M. Niemayer.

Kayser, Wolfgang. 1958. "Wer erzählt den Roman?" In Wolfgang Kayser, *Die Vortragsreise: Studien zur Literatur*, pp. 82–101. Bern: Francke Verlag.

Kerbrat-Orecchioni, Catherine. 1980. *L'Enonciation: De la subjectivité dans le langage*. Paris: Armand Colin.

Kermode, Frank. 1967. *The Sense of an Ending*. New York: Oxford University Press.

Kintsch, Walter, and Teun A. van Dijk. 1975. "Recalling and Summarizing Stories." *Language* 40:98–116.

Kloepfer, Rolf. 1980. "Dynamic Structures in Narrative Literature: 'The Dialogic Principle.' " *Poetics Today* 1:115–34.

Köngäs-Maranda, Elli, and Pierre Maranda. 1971. *Structural Models in Folklore and Transformational Essays*. The Hague: Mouton.

Kristeva, Julia. 1969. *Semeiotikè: Recherches pour une sémanalyse*. Paris: Seuil.

———. 1984. *Revolution in Poetic Language*. Trans. Margaret Waller. New York: Columbia University Press.

Labov, William. 1972. *Language in the Inner City*. Philadelphia: University of Pennsylvania Press.

Labov, William, and Joshua Waletzky. 1967. "Narrative Analysis: Oral Versions of Personal Experience." In June Helm, ed., *Essays on the Verbal and Visual Arts:*

Proceedings of the 1966 Annual Spring Meeting, pp. 12–44. Seattle: University of Washington Press.

Lakoff, George. 1972. "Structural Complexity in Fairy Tales." *Study of Man* 1:128–50.

Lämmert, Eberhart. 1955. *Bauformen des Erzählens.* Stuttgart: J. B. Metzlersche Verlag.

Lanser, Susan Sniader. 1981. *The Narrative Act: Point of View in Fiction.* Princeton: Princeton University Press.

Larivaille, Paul. 1974. "L'Analyse (morpho)logique du récit." *Poétique,* no. 19: 368–88.

Leibfreid, Erwin. 1970. *Kritische Wissenschaft vom Text: Manipulation, Reflexion, transparente Poetologie.* Stuttgart: J. B. Metzler.

Lejeune, Philippe. 1975. *Le Pacte autobiographique.* Paris: Seuil.

———. 1982. "The Autobiographical Contract." In Todorov, *French Literary Theory,* pp. 192–222. *See* Barthes 1982.

Lemon, Lee T., and Marion J. Reis, eds. 1965. *Russian Formalist Criticism.* Lincoln: University of Nebraska Press.

Lévi-Strauss, Claude. 1963. *Structural Anthropology.* Trans. Claire Jacobson and Brooke G. Schoepf. New York: Basic Books.

———. 1965–71. *Mythologiques.* 4 vols. Paris: Plon.

Liddell, Robert. 1947. *A Treatise on the Novel.* London: J. Cape.

Lintvelt, Jaap. 1981. *Essai de typologie narrative: Le 'point de vue.'* Paris: Corti.

Lips, Marguerite. 1926. *Le Style indirect libre.* Paris: Payot.

Lodge, David. 1977. *The Modes of Modern Writing: Metaphor, Metonymy, and the Typology of Literature.* Ithaca: Cornell University Press.

Lorck, Jean Etienne. 1921. *Die erlebte Rede: Eine sprachliche Untersuchung.* Heidelberg: Carl Winter.

Lotman, Jurij. 1977. *The Structure of the Artistic Text.* Trans. Gail Lenhoff and Ronald Vroon. Michigan Slavic Contributions, no. 7. Ann Arbor: University of Michigan.

Lubbock, Percy. 1965. *The Craft of Fiction.* London: Jonathan Cape.

Lyons, John. 1977. *Semantics.* 2 vols. Cambridge: Cambridge University Press.

McHale, Brian. 1978. "Free Indirect Discourse: A Survey of Recent Accounts." *PTL* 3:249–288.

———. 1983. "Unspeakable Sentences, Unnatural Acts: Linguistics and Poetics Revisited." *Poetics Today* 1:17–45.

Madden, David. 1980. *A Primer of the Novel: For Readers and Writers.* Metuchen, N.J.: Scarecrow Press.

Magny, Claude-Edmonde. 1972. *The Age of the American Novel.* Trans. Eleanor Hochman. New York: Ungar.

Malinowski, Bronislaw. 1953. "The Problem of Meaning in Primitive Languages." In C. K. Ogden and I. A. Richards, eds., *The Meaning of Meaning,* pp. 296–336. New York: Oxford University Press.

Mandler, Jean M., and Nancy S. Johnson. 1977. "Remembrance of Things Parsed: Story Structure and Recall." *Cognitive Psychology* 9:11–151.

Margolin, Uri. 1983. "Characterization in Narrative: Some Theoretical Prolegomena." *Neophilologus* 67:1–14.

Martin, Wallace. 1986. *Recent Theories of Narrative.* Ithaca: Cornell University Press.

Martínez-Bonati, Felix. 1981. *Fictive Discourse and the Structure of Literature: A Phenomenological Approach.* Trans. Philip W. Silver. Ithaca: Cornell University Press.

Matejka, Ladislav, and Krỳstyna Pomorska, eds. 1971. *Readings in Russian Poetics.* Cambridge: MIT Press.

Mathieu, Michel. 1974. "Les Acteurs du récit." *Poétique,* no. 19: 357–67.

Mathieu-Colas, Michel. 1986. "Frontières de la narratologie." *Poétique,* no. 65: 91–110.

Mendilow, A. A. 1952. *Time and the Novel.* London: P. Nevill.

Metz, Christian. 1974. *Film Language: A Semiotics of the Cinema.* Trans. Michael Taylor. New York: Oxford University Press.

Miller, D. A. 1981. *Narrative and Its Discontents: Problems of Closure in the Traditional Novel.* Princeton: Princeton University Press.

Mink, Louis O. 1969–70. "History and Fiction as Modes of Comprehension." *New Literary History* 1:541–58.

———. 1978. "Narrative Form as a Cognitive Instrument." In Robert H. Canary and Henry Kozicki, eds., *The Writing of History: Literary Form and Historical Understanding, pp. 129–49.* Madison: University of Wisconsin Press.

Minsky, Marvin. 1975. "A Framework for Representing Knowledge." In Patrick Winston, ed., *The Psychology of Computer Vision,* pp. 211–77. New York: McGraw-Hill.

Mitchell, W.J.T., ed. 1981. *On Narrative.* Chicago: University of Chicago Press.

Morgan, Thaïs E. 1985. "Is There an Intertext in This Text? Literary and Interdisciplinary Approaches to Intertextuality." *American Journal of Semiotics* 3:1–40.

Morrissette, Bruce. 1965. "Narrative 'You' in Contemporary Literature," *Comparative Literature Studies* 2:1–24.

Mosher, Harold F. 1980. "A New Synthesis of Narratology." *Poetics Today* 1:171–86.

Müller, Günther. 1968. *Morphologische Poetik.* Tubingen: Max Niemeyer.

O'Grady, Walter. 1965. "On Plot in Modern Fiction: Hardy, James, and Conrad." *Modern Fiction Studies* 11:107–15.

Page, Norman. 1973. *Speech in the English Novel.* London: Longman.

Palmer, F. R. 1971. *Semantics.* 2d ed. Cambridge: Cambridge University Press.

Pascal, Roy. 1962. "Tense and Novel." *Modern Language Review* 57:1–11.

———. 1977. *The Dual Voice: Free Indirect Speech and Its Functioning in the Nineteenth-Century European Novel.* Manchester: Manchester University Press.

Pavel, Thomas. 1976. *La Syntaxe narrative des tragédies de Corneille.* Paris: Klincksieck.

———. 1980. "Narrative Domains." *Poetics Today* 1:105–14.

———. 1985. *The Poetics of Plot: The Case of English Renaissance Drama.* Minneapolis: University of Minnesota Press.

Piaget, Jean. 1970. *Structuralism.* Trans. Chaninah Maschler. New York: Basic Books.

Pike, Kenneth L. 1967. *Language in Relation to a Unified Theory of the Structure of Human Behavior.* The Hague: Mouton.

Piwowarczyk, Mary Ann. 1976. "The Narratee and the Situation of Enunciation: A Reconsideration of Prince's Theory." *Genre* 9:161–77.

Plato. 1968. *The Republic.* Trans. Allan Bloom. New York: Basic Books.

Polanyi, Livia. 1979. "So What's the Point?" *Semiotica* 25:207–41.

Pottier, Bernard. 1964. "Vers une sémantique moderne." *Travaux de linguistique et de littérature* 2:107–37.

Pouillon, Jean. 1946. *Temps et roman.* Paris: Gallimard.

Pratt, Mary Louise. 1977. *Toward a Speech Act Theory of Literary Discourse.* Bloomington: Indiana University Press.

Prince, Gerald. 1973. *A Grammar of Stories.* The Hague: Mouton.

———. 1977. "Remarques sur les signes métanarratifs." *Degrés,* nos. 11–12:e1–e10.

———. 1978. "Le Discours attributif et le récit." *Poétique,* no. 35:305–13.

———. 1980. "Introduction to the Study of the Narratee." In Jane P. Tompkins, ed., *Reader-Response Criticism,* pp. 7–25. Baltimore: Johns Hopkins University Press.

———. 1981. "Reading and Narrative Competence." *L'Esprit Créateur* 21:81–88.

———. 1981–82. "Narrative Analysis and Narratology." *New Literary History* 13:179–88.

———. 1982. *Narratology: The Form and Functioning of Narrative.* Berlin: Mouton.

———. 1983. "Narrative Pragmatics, Message, and Point." *Poetics* 12:527–36.

———. 1985. "Thématiser." *Poétique,* no. 64:425–33.

Propp, Vladimir. 1968. *Morphology of the Folktale.* 2d ed. Trans. Laurence Scott. Austin: University of Texas Press.

———. 1984. "Transformations of the Wondertale." In Vladimir Propp, *Theory and History of Folklore,* pp. 82–99. Ed. Anatoly Liberman. Trans. Ariadna Y. Martin and Richard P. Martin. Minneapolis: University of Minnesota Press.

Rabinowitz, Peter. 1977. "Truth in Fiction: A Reexamination of Audiences." *Critical Inquiry* 4:121–41.

Rabkin, Eric S. 1973. *Narrative Suspense: "When Slim Turned Sideways . . . ."* Ann Arbor: University of Michigan Press.

Rastier, François. 1973. *Essais de sémiotique discursive.* Tours: Mame.

Ricardou, Jean. 1967. *Problèmes du nouveau roman.* Paris: Seuil.

———. 1971. *Pour une théorie du nouveau roman.* Paris: Seuil.

———. 1973. *Le Nouveau Roman.* Paris: Seuil.

———. 1978. *Nouveaux Problèmes du roman.* Paris: Seuil.

Richards, I. A. 1950. *Practical Criticism: A Study of Literary Judgment.* New York: Harcourt, Brace.

Ricoeur, Paul. 1984. *Time and Narrative.* Vol. 1. Trans. Kathleen McLaughlin and David Pellauer. Chicago: University of Chicago Press.

———. 1985. *Time and Narrative.* Vol. 2. Trans. Kathleen McLaughlin and David Pellauer. Chicago: University of Chicago Press.

Riffaterre, Michael. 1972. "Système d'un genre descriptif." *Poétique,* no. 9:15–30.

——. 1972–73. "Interpretation and Descriptive Poetry." *New Literary History* 4:229–56.

——. 1978. *Semiotics of Poetry.* Bloomington: Indiana University Press.

——. 1980. "La Trace de l'intertexte." *La Pensée,* no. 215:4–18.

——. 1983. *Text Production.* Trans. Terese Lyons. New York: Columbia University Press.

Rimmon, Shlomith. 1976. "A Comprehensive Theory of Narrative: Genette's *Figures III* and the Structuralist Study of Fiction." *PTL* 1:33–62.

Rimmon-Kenan, Shlomith. 1983. *Narrative Fiction: Contemporary Poetics.* London: Methuen.

——. 1985. "Qu'est-ce qu'un thème?" *Poétique,* no. 64:397–406.

Rogers, B. G. 1965. *Proust's Narrative Techniques.* Geneva: Droz.

Romberg, Bertil. 1962. *Studies in the Narrative Technique of First-Person Novel.* Lund: Almqvist & Wiksell.

van Rossum-Guyon, Françoise. 1970. "Point de vue ou perspective narrative." *Poétique,* no. 4:476–97.

Rousset, Jean. 1973. *Narcisse romancier: Essai sur la première personne dans le roman.* Paris: Corti.

Rumelhart, David E. 1975. "Notes on a Schema for Stories." In Daniel G. Bobrow and Allan Collins, eds., *Representation and Understanding: Studies in Cognitive Science,* pp. 211–36. New York: Academic Press.

Ryan, Marie-Laure. 1979. "Linguistic Models in Narratology." *Semiotica* 28:127–55.

——. 1981. "The Pragmatics of Personal and Impersonal Fiction." *Poetics* 10:517–39.

——. 1984. "Fiction as a Logical, Ontological, and Illocutionary Issue," *Style* 18:121–39.

——. 1985. "The Modal Structure of Narrative Universes." *Poetics Today* 6:717–55.

Sacks, Harvey. 1972. "On the Analyzability of Stories by Children." In John J. Gumperz and Dell Hymes, eds., *Directions in Sociolinguistics,* pp. 325–45. New York: Holt, Rinehart and Winston.

Said, Edward. 1975. *Beginnings: Intention and Method.* New York: Basic Books.

Sartre, Jean-Paul. 1965. *What Is Literature?* Trans. Bernard Frechtman. New York: Harper & Row.

Saussure, Ferdinand de. 1966. *Course in General Linguistics.* Trans. Wade Baskin. New York: McGraw-Hill.

Schank, Roger. 1975. "The Structure of Episodes in Memory." In Daniel G. Bobrow and Allan Collins, eds., *Representation and Understanding: Studies in Cognitive Science,* pp. 237–72. New York: Academic Press.

Schank, Roger, and Robert Abelson. 1977. *Scripts, Plans, Goals, and Understanding.* Hillsdale, N.J.: Lawrence Erlbaum Associates.

Schmid, Wolf. 1973. *Der Textaufbau in den Erzählungen Dostoevskijs.* Munich: Fink.

Scholes, Robert. 1974. *Structuralism in Literature: An Introduction.* New Haven: Yale University Press.

Scholes, Robert, and Robert Kellogg. 1966.

The Nature of Narrative. New York: Oxford University Press.

Searle, John. 1969. *Speech Acts.* Cambridge: Cambridge University Press.

———. 1975. "Indirect Speech Acts." In Peter Coles and Jerry L. Morgan, eds., *Syntax and Semantics III: Speech Acts,* pp. 59–82. New York: Academic Press.

———. 1976. "A Classification of Illocutionary Acts." *Language in Society* 5:1–23.

Segre, Cesare. 1979. *Structure and Time: Narration, Poetry, Models.* Trans. John Meddemmen. Chicago: University of Chicago Press.

Shapiro, Marianne. 1984. "How Narrators Report Speech." *Language and Style* 17:67–78.

Shklovsky, Victor. 1965a. "Art as Technique." In Lemon and Reis 1965, pp. 3–24.

———. 1965b. "Sterne's *Tristram Shandy:* Stylistic Commentary." Ibid., pp. 25–57.

Smith, Barbara Herrnstein. 1968. *Poetic Closure: A Study of How Poems End.* Chicago: University of Chicago Press.

———. 1981. "Narrative Versions, Narrative Theories." In W.J.T. Mitchell, ed., *On Narrative,* pp. 209–32. Chicago: University of Chicago Press.

Souriau, Etienne. 1950. *Les Deux Cent Mille Situations dramatiques.* Paris: Flammarion.

Souvage, Jacques. 1965. *An Introduction to the Study of the Novel, with Special Reference to the English Novel.* Ghent: E. Story-Scientia P.V.B.A.

Spitzer, Leo. 1928. "Zum Stil Marcel Proust." *Stilstudien II,* pp. 365–497. Munich: Max Hueber.

Stanzel, Franz. 1964. *Typische Formen des Roman.* Göttingen: Vandenhoeck & Ruprecht.

———. 1971. *Narrative Situations in the Novel: "Tom Jones," "Moby-Dick," "The Ambassadors," "Ulysses."* Trans. James P. Pusack. Bloomington: Indiana University Press.

———. 1984. *A Theory of Narrative.* Trans. Charlotte Goedsche. Cambridge: Cambridge University Press.

Stein, Nancy L. 1982. "The Definition of a Story," *Journal of Pragmatics* 6:487–507.

Steinberg, Gunter. 1971. *Erlebte Rede: Ihre Eigenart und ihre Formen in neuerer deutscher, französischer und englischer Erzählliteratur.* 2 vols. Göppingen: A. Kümmerle.

Sternberg, Meir. 1974. "What Is Exposition?" In John Halperin, ed., *The Theory of the Novel.* New York: Oxford University Press.

———. 1978. *Expositional Modes and Temporal Ordering in Fiction.* Baltimore: Johns Hopkins University Press.

Strauch, Gérard. 1974. "De quelques interprétations récentes du style indirect libre." *Recherches Anglaises et Américaines* 7:40–73.

Suleiman, Susan R. 1980. "Redundancy and the 'Readable' Text." *Poetics Today* 1:119–42.

———. 1983. *Authoritarian Fictions: The Ideological Novel as a Literary Genre.* New York: Columbia University Press.

Tacca, Oscar. 1973. *Las Voces de la novela.* Madrid: Editorial Grados.

Tamir, Nomi. 1976. "Personal Narration and

Its Linguistic Foundation." *PTL* 1:403–29.

Thorndyke, Perry W. 1977. "Cognitive Structures in Comprehension and Memory of Narrative Discourse." *Cognitive Psychology* 9:77–110.

Tillotson, Kathleen. 1959. *The Tale and the Teller*. London: Rupert Hart-Davis.

Titunik, Irwin Robert. 1963. *The Problem of 'Skaz' in Russian Literature*. Ph.D. thesis, University of California—Berkeley. Reproduced by microfilm-xerography by University Microfilms International, 1976.

Todorov, Tzvetan. 1966. "Les Catégories du récit littéraire." *Communications*, no. 8: 125–51.

———. 1969. *Grammaire du "Décaméron."* The Hague: Mouton.

———. 1978. *The Poetics of Prose*. Trans. Richard Howard. Ithaca: Cornell University Press.

———. 1981. *Introduction to Poetics*. Trans. Richard Howard. Minneapolis: University of Minnesota Press.

Tomashevsky, Boris. 1965. "Thematics." In Lemon and Reis 1965, pp. 61–95.

Torgovnick, Marianna. 1981. *Closure in the Novel*. Princeton: Princeton University Press.

Uspenskij, Boris. *A Poetics of Composition: The Structure of the Artistic Text and Typology of a Compositional Form*. Trans. Valentina Zavarin and Susan Wittig. Berkeley and Los Angeles: University of California Press.

Vinogradov, V. V. 1980. "The Problem of *Skaz* in Stylistics." In Ellendea Proffer and Carl R. Proffer, eds., *The Ardis Anthology of Russian Futurism*. Ann Arbor: Ardis.

Vitoux, Pierre. 1982. "Le Jeu de la focalisation." *Poétique,* no. 51:359–68.

Vološinov, V. N. 1973. *Marxism and the Philosophy of Language*. Trans. Ladislav Matejka and I. R. Titunik. New York: Seminar Press.

Weimann, Robert. 1973. "Point of View in Fiction." In Gaylord C. Leroy and Ursula Beitz, eds., *Preserve and Create: Essays in Marxist Literary Criticism,* pp. 54–75. New York: Humanities Press.

Weinrich, Harald. 1964. *Tempus, Besprochene und Erzählte Welt*. Stuttgart: W. Kohlhammer.

Wellek, René, and Austin Warren. 1949. *Theory of Literature*. New York: Harcourt, Brace.

White, Hayden. 1973. *Metahistory: The Historical Imagination in Nineteenth Century Europe*. Baltimore: Johns Hopkins University Press.

Wilensky, Robert. 1978. *Understanding Goal-Based Stories*. Research Report no. 140, Department of Computer Science, Yale University, New Haven.

Winograd, Terry. 1975. "Frame Representations and the Declarative-Procedural Controversy." In Daniel G. Bobrow and Allan Collins, eds., *Representation and Understanding: Studies in Cognitive Science,* pp. 185–210. New York: Academic Press.

Wittmann, Henri. 1975. "Théorie des narrèmes et algorithmes narratifs." *Poetics* 4:19–28.

Wright, Austin. 1982. *The Formal Principle in the Novel*. Ithaca: Cornell University Press.

Wright, Terence. 1985. "Rhythm in the

Novel." *Modern Language Review* 80:1–
15.

Zeraffa, Michel. 1969. *Personne et personnage.* Paris: Klincksieck.

Zholkovsky, Alexander. 1984. *Themes and
Texts: Toward a Poetics of Expressive-
ness.* Translated by the author and
edited by Kathleen Parté. Ithaca: Cornell
University Press.

Zoran, Gabriel. 1984. "Towards a Theory of
Space in Narrative." *Poetics Today*
5:309–35.

118